INTERACTION IN MULTIDISCIPLINARY TEAMS

Cardiff Papers in Qualitative Research

About the Series

The Cardiff School of Social Sciences at Cardiff University is well known for the breadth and quality of its empirical research in various major areas of sociology and social policy. In particular, it enjoys an international reputation for research using qualitative methodology, including qualitative approaches to data collection and analysis.

This series publishes original sociological research that reflects the tradition of qualitative and ethnographic inquiry developed at Cardiff in recent years. The series includes monographs reporting on empirical research, collections of papers reporting on particular themes and other monographs or edited collections on methodological developments and issues.

Interaction in Multidisciplinary Teams

WILLIAM HOUSLEY
School of Social Sciences
Cardiff University, UK

ASHGATE

Published by
Ashgate Publishing Limited
Gower House
Croft Road
Aldershot
Hants GU11 3HR
England

Ashgate Publishing Company
Suite 420
101 Cherry Street
Burlington, VT 05401-4405
USA

Ashgate website: http://www.ashgate.com

British Library Cataloguing in Publication Data
Housley, William
    Interaction in multidisciplinary teams. - (Cardiff papers
    in qualitative research)
    1.Social service - Teamwork 2.Interprofessional relations
    3.Social interaction
    I.Title II.Cardiff University. School of Social Sciences
    361.3'2

Library of Congress Cataloging-in-Publication Data
Housley, William, 1970-
    Interaction in multidisciplinary teams / William Housley.
        p.cm. -- (Cardiff papers in qualitative research)   -
    Includes bibliographical references.
    ISBN 0-7546-1796-3 (alk. paper)
    1.Social service--Teamwork. 2. Teams in the workplace. I. Title. II. Series.

    HV41 .H667 2002
    361.3--dc21

                                                        2002025872

ISBN 0 7546 1796 3

Printed and bound in Great Britain by Antony Rowe Ltd.,
Chippenham, Wiltshire

Contents

Acknowledgements

I would like to thank Jackie Swift for her help with the preparation of the manuscript and my colleagues at the School of Social Sciences, Cardiff University. I would also like to thank the ESRC for their support of the postgraduate research from which some of this work is derived.

For Michelle

1 Bringing the Multidisciplinary into Team

Introduction

During the course of this book I will attempt to make some observations about professional practice within social work/care work teams. These observations are drawn from ethnographic, ethnomethodological and discourse analytic research into multidisciplinary social/care work team practice. The research investigated the interactional dynamics of a number of theoretically sampled multidisciplinary social/care work teams. The book attempts to report and bring together a number of observations generated during the course of this project. In order to do this I will first explore some of the ideas concerning multidisciplinarity and team work. This is followed by a discussion of my observations on multidisciplinary team practice. These observations will be relayed through the use of some illustrative examples of talk and interaction gathered from a case study of one of the multidisciplinary teams that the research examined. During the concluding chapter of this book I will reflect on some issues facing the development and promotion of multidisciplinarity within team based settings.

Multidisciplinarity

At the core of the conceptual apparatus of multidisciplinarity is the concept of knowledge and it's social organisation. The concept of multidisciplinarity is one that is grounded within a functionalist and systems based account of the social organisation of knowledge. The systems oriented organisation of knowledge in this way is seen as crucial to the efficiency and utility of knowledge systems in solving human problems. Furthermore, knowledge within Western societies has been subject to fragmentation (Kline 1995), multidisciplinarity, as a systems based concept, is an attempt to overcome fragmented thinking and develop holistic modes of enquiry, decision making and practice (Kline 1995). The systems approach towards knowledge has, through various histories of science, the philosophy of Kuhn (1962) and Popper (1902-1989), promoted a view of knowledge systems as functional entities subject to organisational and homeostatic tendencies. Furthermore, the heterogeneity of human knowledge, due to historical and social factors, had been seen to produce a fractured picture of the world within which holistic solutions to human problems had not been forthcoming. The notion of holistic truth is one that can be understood to emerge from the notion of universal truth. However, holistic truth is an attempt to draw the sting of relativism by accounting for the diversity of truths-in-the-world while universal truth is seen as an outmoded attempt to establish epistemological security that has resulted in problematic consequences for domains popularised by the new narratives of ecology, anti-racism, feminism, psychotherapy, info-technology and mysticism. Furthermore, the way in which knowledge bases and activities were *organised* can be seen to be one of the ways through which this failure has reproduced itself through social practices. Consequently, we may understand how attempts to ameliorate the organisation and practice of knowledge have provided for the emergence of the multidisciplinary approach that can be understood in terms of the theoretical context described. Kline (1995: 1) recognises this in her introduction to the book *Conceptual Foundations for Multidisciplinary Thinking* within which she states:

> The intellectual system erected largely in the western world since the Reformation is enormously powerful and productive. Although we may have much yet to learn, the scientific approach to knowledge since the time of Galileo has provided the human race with a far better understanding of our world and of ourselves than was available to any previous society. This gain in understanding has arisen primarily from two sources. We have adopted what we loosely call 'scientific methods,' and we have broken the intellectual enterprise into larger and larger number of parts (disciplines and research programs). We have created working groups of scholars who study each of the parts in as 'scientific' a method they can bring to bear. However, there is a near total absence of overview of the intellectual terrain.

Despite the euro-centric assumptions of this statement, the questionable portrayal of progress and the categorisation of Western knowledge as indicative of a scientistic form of life, it displays an initial assumption through which the merits of multidisciplinarity has been substantiated. In terms of Kline's work, multidisciplinarity is a systems solution to the lack of a holistic approach to the present intellectual terrain. The systems analogy is one familiar to students of Parsonian functionalism

(Parsons 1956). This analogy was adopted by structural functionalism from cybernetics, a sub-discipline of engineering, in order to illustrate the way in which social systems exhibited forms of complexity characterised by self regulating tendencies in the form of positive and negative feedback mechanisms and self sustaining replicating processes. The adoption of such an approach will, in terms of the humanist march of progress thesis adopted by Kline, improve our lot. The differences between disciplines are viewed as inhibitors to a fuller understanding of the world and our place in it. In short Kline seeks to indulge in some 'knowledge engineering' through which the separateness of disciplines is overcome. This, she argues, involves the construction of a multidisciplinary discourse through which disciplines can effectively engage with each other. The benefits of such a strategy, she argues, would ultimately be more effective solutions to human problems.

Kline proposes some rules of multidisciplinary thinking (1995:274). She suggests that in order to achieve multidisciplinarity a discourse must be established, a set of language games with rules and practices formed, and cognitive engineering (i.e. the development of various schemata, cognitive aids and logic) in the form of what are described as 'sysreps' (1995:30) initiated. The notion of 'sysreps' is understood as a series of system representations. That is to say devices, which may be heuristic in form, which can be operationalised as a means of establishing the cognitive basis for a desired discursive framework to take root. In essence, Kline is proposing a new grammar or categorial order through which the marriage of intellectual work and human 'progress' can be reinvigorated for the good of humanity (Kline 1995).

These ambitions are no doubt worthy and laudable. However, we are being presented with a categorial order, a set of concepts and practices that are, like a grammar, constructed according to rules and theoretically devised conventions. Furthermore, Kline's categorial order describes intellectual endeavour in terms of 'parts' and 'wholes' and is indicative of a systems approach. That is to say, Kline views knowledge as a set of systems. Different disciplines are conceptualised as systems of knowledge that we do not or cannot always perceive in terms of a meta-system or an overall view. She argues that one of the reasons for using the system concept is due to its existence (i.e. use) in many branches of scientific endeavour (Kline 1995:15). Knowledge in the form of disciplines is, according to Kline, in the business of making truth assertions and the system concept is central to establishing 'truth'. Indeed the whole process of making truth assertions is viewed as essentially systemic in nature. Therefore, the rules of multidisciplinarity (the grammar or categorial order) must take account of the way in which systems are used as a tool for establishing 'truth'. Kline refers to the practices of classification and the formulation of rules and testing as examples of the ways through which disciplines deal with systems in the process of establishing truth claims (1995:199,200). According to Kline, this is done by using systems as a mirror with which to compare assertions to the systemic model. In this sense truth assertions, as Popper (1959) noted, can only be disproved rather than proved and for Kline this is representative of the systemic approach to constructing knowledge. Kline continues by noting that disciplines, as distinct systems, produce 'truth' but not the whole truth. Thus, her categorial order for realising multidisciplinarity, once 'run' like a software program on the hardware of the human brain and society, must integrate the various disciplines' approaches to similar phenomena in order to achieve holistic explanation and understanding.

Having covered these points we can now understand how multidisciplinarity is viewed as a solution to the problem of compartmentalised knowledge and other 'inefficiencies' within the socio-technical plenum. To this extent whilst I do not wish to provide a full discursive genealogy of multidisciplinarity it is worth noting, in theoretical terms, the orientations and assumptions which characterise this particular discourse.

We may view it as a systems theory application to a myriad of social, interactive and (other) phenomena. It can be understood as a form of synecdoche i.e. the application of general schema to particular circumstances. Furthermore, Kline's project is explicitly discursive and concerned with engineering language games and cognitive competencies that will facilitate the objective of realising multidisciplinary knowledge construction, pedagogy and the establishment of the 'whole truth'.

Having delineated some of the discursive characteristics of the concept of multidisciplinarity I will now seek to review some of the ways in which this concept was married to notions of teamworking within social care and health settings.

Bringing the Multidisciplinary into Team

The application of the concept of multidisciplinarity to team practice can be viewed as an adaptation of some of the principle theoretical concerns that Kline advances. It is through the breaking down of barriers between disciplines that the grail of holistic truth can be sought. In terms of working in the best interests of the client, the orientation to holistic truth can be seen to be tied to the notion of providing holistic solutions in meeting clients needs and organising structures for meeting such objectives. One of the ways in which this was considered to be possible was by conflating the concept of the 'team' together with the concept of multidisciplinarity. My concerns are not with the history of social/care work as such, but lie in the theoretical (and hence discursive) recommendations and descriptions of how multidisciplinary social work and health care teams are organised and how they function. The discursive link between multidisciplinarity and team working is characterised by three concepts that are central to this process. These are knowledge, communication, interactional structures and roles. I will now consider each of these in turn.

Knowledge

The notion of there being specialised species of knowledge is one that is difficult to pin down in theoretical terms. However, important social theoretical notions of 'knowledge' have included an array of concepts provided through the work of Michael Foucault (1976) and, more recently, Bourdieu's concept of cultural capital and embodiment (1990). Alongside these concepts we may place the Schutzian notion of the 'stock of commonsense knowledge', although 'knowledge' can also be understood as a set of ideas which have powerful explanatory force. Kline's (1995) concern with developing a grammar for multidisciplinarity as a means of reaching the goal of more 'holistic truth assertions' can be seen to be mirrored in theoretical commentaries of multidisciplinarity with respect to social work and care practice. Thus, the identification of 'knowledge' and 'disciplines' is also a crucial starting point for those wishing to apply a grammar of multidisciplinarity to rearranging the organisation of social work as a means of improving decision making and ultimately more efficiently meeting the needs of clients. 'Holistic truth' is viewed as approximating to a reservoir of multidisciplinary knowledge which can be tapped to provide holistic solutions to social work organisation and practice.

The identification of professions with access to a privileged 'knowledge base' or a 'specialised form of knowledge' is one which is confirmed within much sociological literature (e.g. Foucault 1973, 1976). The emergence of social institutions is also viewed as an important historical development in accounting for the emergence of professions grounded on claims to privileged sources of knowledge. As Clarke (1994:14) states:

> ... such (institutional) developments emphasised the necessity of creating recognisable clusters of professional 'expertise' for welfare services,

especially given the relative lack of relevant training and qualifications. Equally, the expansion and creation of nationally organised frameworks for service delivery created the conditions for further professional development.

In the case of social work, for example, the 'growth of an expertise' (Sapsford 1995:23) has been located in terms of historical processes and the professionalisation of various activities within the rubric of 'social work'. However, social work (as an example of the relationship between profession and knowledge) has been seen as a case study for the examination of the formation of a diverse knowledge base drawing from a number of different sources. Whilst 'doctors' and 'nurses' are viewed as conforming to a 'medical model', social work, according to Butrym and Horder (1983:10):

> ...relies for its theoretical base on knowledge borrowed from a variety of disciplines, particularly the Social Sciences...(Others) fail to appreciate the intellectual autonomy, creativeness and challenge in the selection and application of knowledge.

Changes in social work have shifted from specialist social work to generic social work and the profession is now being challenged by the growth of care management. However, such changes will not be focussed upon although from a historical approach they are important. Despite these changes, the connection between social workers (as professionals) and a knowledge base is viewed as tremendously important. More recently Coulshead (1991:8) states:

> Social Work theory... should serve the following functions: it should provide some explanation for the complexities we observe in our practice so that out of apparent chaos we might expose patterns and regularities in behaviour and situations: it should therefore help us to predict future behaviour, and how the problem or condition could develop and what might be the effect of planned change.

Clearly the claim being made here is that social work knowledge should draw upon theoretical principles and a knowledge base, established through observational criteria, which can provide for predictability. Thus, the validity of social work 'knowledge' is achieved through its perceived accuracy and utility in predicting events. To this extent, social work knowledge is being contextualised in terms of scientistic aspirations. However, in recent years the notion of 'multidisciplinarity' has been invoked as a means of providing more informed and sensitive care for clients. The notion of multidisciplinarity is, as we have seen, derived from a number of theoretical ideas in the human sciences. Kline (1995:2) describes multidisciplinary study as that which:

> ...examines the appropriate relationships of the disciplines to each other and the larger intellectual terrain.

From a social work point of view the construction of a knowledge base from various sources perhaps makes the adoption of a multidisciplinary approach within social work discourse a logical development. Echoing Kline's conceptualisation of multidisciplinary study, the HMSO *Report of the Working Party on Social Workers in Local authority Health and Welfare Services* (HMSO 1959) states:

> In view of the fast growing complexity and scope of modern knowledge no one can profession dealing with a range of human needs can make exclusive claim in relation to others, each has its essential functions as well as its necessary overlap with others.

Furthermore, the appropriation of 'multidisciplinary work' within social work terminology is not only viewed as a means of providing a more holistic view with which to inform social work practice. Indeed it is viewed as a means of dealing more effectively with 'clients needs' which, being 'subjective phenomena', are met more effectively by a diverse body of knowledge rather than monolithic models of social behaviour. As Hey and Marshall (1979:25) state:

> The contributions of a number of different professions are called for if citizens are to obtain the individual services they need and if the services are to be delivered in co-ordinated and sensible ways. Close collaboration between professions is often necessary if effective help is to be given.

It is from this position that the notion of 'multidisciplinary teams' was derived. This was seen to be a means of realising some of the objectives and considerations mentioned previously. In short, multidisciplinarity was viewed as a means of establishing a holistic approach to social welfare knowledge construction and practice utilising the institutional vehicle of the 'team' contextualised within the discourse of group organicism.

Despite this a more thorough going conceptualisation of professional knowledge is not forthcoming. Critiques of the psychological base of much social welfare knowledge (Sapsford 1995:39) and concerns with the way in which it deploys a pathological model of explaining social problems, the actual 'use of this knowledge' within team practice is left, largely, to theoretical speculation. Furthermore, from an ethnomethodological point of view such speculation and theoretical inference serves to miss the interactional 'what' of multidisciplinary team practice (Housley, 1999).

Communicative and Interactional Structure

The social organisation of multidisciplinary teams is seen to be crucial if the objectives discussed above are to be brought bare on the business of meeting clients' needs. According to Evers (1981:209) one of the principles of these teams was to function in a way where:

> ...collaboration was seen to be achieved through mutual accommodation and exchange of information amongst a company of equals, each contributing on the basis of their authoritative knowledge and expertise...

This process of collaboration and communication is seen to be of prime importance to the decision making process within teams. Indeed, social work discourse notes the problems of differences in 'status' between professions. Questions of status have been discussed by a number of social work and health commentators (e.g. Donnison 1977, Salvage 1985). The problem of differential status is understood to be connected to the different status of different modes of expertise and the knowledge base from which they are drawn from. Thus as Hunt and Marshall (1979:15) put it:

> ... integrating members of different status...[is] a major stumbling block in many interdisciplinary team efforts... Explicit status distinctions in a group tend to reduce the interaction and social support among members.

Consequently 'status' is seen as one of the principle issues which need to be accommodated for in the organisation of multidisciplinary teams. Further work on the organisation of multidisciplinary teams has been occupied with the business of 'making them work'. Ramcharan (1993) provides the example of McGrath's work (1991) which is seen to exhibit such 'pragmatic' considerations, however according to Ramcharan (1993:163) whilst McGrath:

> ...reviews a vast literature and proposes a number of features of such Teams which, from the literature, are taken to be positive in terms of their functioning... the evidence is difficult to interpret, and is further compounded by the lack of empirical research.

Despite the lack of empirical research Øvreveit (1993) suggests that communication is a vital aspect of 'good teamwork'. For Øvretveit, communication problems within teams may be due to different professions and agencies 'confidentiality and disclosure policies' which may 'hamper good communications'. However, Øvretveit notes that *modes* of communication within the team are also important in ameliorating communication problems.

For Øvretveit, 'information, meaning and dialogue' are vital to effective team communications and decision making. Øvretveit considers this process to be centred about the 'sending' and 'receiving' information. Øvretveit (1993:161-2) states:

> The simple part of improving communications is to arrange ways to send, receive, record and retrieve basic factual information quickly, easily and accurately. Here I mean the sort of information which is specific and not open to interpretation. For this a team needs a basic communications and records system such as the one discussed later, to send, receive and store verbal and written information. The more difficult part of improving communications is how to improve exchanging and understanding meanings. This involves 'reaching out' to the receiver and exchanging perceptions. Sending and receiving information in this type of communication is for exploring and creating meaning and significance - it is more about dialogue and a meeting of minds than about transmitting or exchanging facts.

Whilst Øvretveit provides no empirical evidence to support this model, it is nevertheless confidently advanced. The notion of a 'meeting of minds' may be a useful explanatory metaphor. However, it remains a highly unspecified figure of speech. How minds might meet is not explained and such a process has no empirical or observational foundations. Consequently, Øvretveit casually glosses over a complex and difficult process through the use of a vague phrase. Øvretveit's reference to 'dialogue' perhaps refers to a specific set of processes, but it remains a vague description of the interactional work carried out within teams. Indeed, Øvretveit's main focus is with communication issues such as the flow of documentary information, confidentiality, professional practices and team members' access to information. Whilst Øvretveit refers to 'dialogue', it is not developed or examined despite its description as a vital aspect of team communication and organisation, it is often signified as a line or collection of lines within Øvretveit's copious flowcharts, schema and diagrams of multidisciplinary team organisation.

Role and Identity as Structural Components of the 'Multidisciplinary Team'

The concept of role (or rather references to the category of role) is prominent in accounts of effective multidisciplinary teamwork and organisation. As Brill (1976:86) states:

> The comment is frequently encountered in literature on teamwork that the effectiveness of the Team is dependent on how clearly the boundaries of the various specialities can be defined and their roles explicated. It is also pointed out that many of the major conflicts between team members arise not out of personality problems but out of lack of role definition that is understood and accepted. it seems inevitable that there will be a certain amount of role overlap, except in those instances where the content of the speciality is very specific. This means that role negotiation must be continuous and on going, and the effective team creates a climate where this can be maximized and where there is freedom to use unique talents of team members without regard to speciality.

Thus, the organisation of the team must take into account distinctions and the organisation of role as a means of ensuring effective functioning whilst at the same time avoiding problems connected to issues of professional status and different knowledge bases. The precise means by which 'role' is negotiated is not specified, however the interactional dimension of 'role' suggests that communication and *interaction* are, from the theorists point of view, important.

Glastonbury, Bradley and Orme (1987) view teamwork within multidisciplinary settings as necessarily hierarchical in terms of team organisation, functioning and management. As Jacques (1978:87) states with reference to a Brunel University study of child guidance:

> ... another idea that often appears to be taken for granted is that 'team work' necessarily carries with it the condition of absolute parity of status amongst members of a team, and more particularly that no one has authority over anyone else... often the myth of equality is confronted with the reality of the dominant role of one particular member.

For Glastonbury et al, such hierarchical organisation is also provided for by the emergence of role specific terms within the arena of 'effective management'. This involves the concepts of 'key worker', 'leader' and 'co-ordinator'. They argue that such terms are relatively interchangeable. However, they provide for a general *explanatory taxonomy of role specific ideal types*. Such a taxonomy does not explicitly disown notions of structure, but the focus is oriented to the interactive framework of team work within multidisciplinary social work settings. For Glastonbury et al (ibid) the production of a 'model oriented' approach is characterised through the following terms and notions:

> ... the term 'team' is used to refer to a multidisciplinary team. It emphasises two features of these teams. First, the importance of relationships to the purpose of the group: relationships both between a client and a team member, and between members and each other. these relationships are not secondary to the goal of the team, as they are in some project teams in industry, but are the means through which these relationships are different in different types of team. The second feature is that the combination of team members' efforts is greater than the sum of each persons contribution. A team is a way of co-ordinating each person's efforts so that the final result is of a different order than the sum of each person's efforts.

Clearly the definition of 'team' here is akin to other categories of social structure. Consequently, the view that the team is something that is 'more than the sum of its parts' exhibits a clear and resounding Durkheimian resonance, in the sense that the notion of team is utilised as a means of describing a specific mode of social organisation. Furthermore, it is a means through which individuals' 'efforts' are translated into qualitatively improved level of 'work'. The team magnifies individual contributions and is thus conceptualised as an 'efficiency gain' structure, therefore the team is contextualised in terms of systems theory which exhibits the view that systems are a more efficient way of tackling specific goals in comparison to isolated individual effort. The 'sum being more than its parts' argument is one which is deeply entrenched within the sociological project. However, it is often used as a means of glossing over the fine interactional detail and processes which underpin descriptions of the sum, which is usually described in terms of the social or wider society with the parts being the family, educational institutions, the polity and so forth. Whilst the 'team' can be understood as a manifestation of social organisation we can see here how it is being used within a functionalist mode of explanation, a *categorial order,* that reintroduces the structural functionalist model by substituting team members as *parts* of the *sum*; in this case the team represents the *sum* rather than the social system.

Multidisciplinary Teamwork: Problems and Issues

Recent work within the area of multidisciplinarity and teamwork has extended to healthcare settings with the establishment of primary healthcare teams in England and local healthcare groups in Wales. Both seek to develop and promote a multidisciplinary focus. The merits of teamwork within Primary Health Care settings has been noted by a number of NHS documents (NHSME, 1993). For example, it has been noted that the use of team working within primary healthcare settings allied with principles of multidisciplinarity have produced positive health care outcomes and the meeting of patient needs (West and Slater 1996, Wood, Farrow and Eliot 1994).

However, despite these positive observations a number of problems surrounding multidisciplinarity and primary health care teamwork have been noted. These echo many of the issues relating to problems described by social workers researchers investigating similar contexts. For example, West and Slater (1996:17) note that an earlier study by Field and West (1995) (that used data generated through 96 interviews of members of primary health care teams) referred:

> [to] a number of factors which impact upon team working in primary health care including structured time for team decision-making, personality and status, group decision making, team cohesiveness and team building [and] the failure of primary health care teams to set aside time for regular meetings to define objectives, clarify roles, apportion tasks, encourage participation and handle change. Other reasons for poor teamwork include differences in status, power, educational background, assertiveness of members of the team, and the assumption that the GP's will be the leaders. They also pinpoint the lack of preparation or support for GP's to take on management roles.

Further work in this area has explored ways of measuring effectiveness of primary healthcare. Through the use of a questionnaire and responses of 137 individuals working within multidisciplinary primary health care teams Pearson and Spencer (1995) pinpoint four specific areas that were understood to be important in measuring and understanding the effectiveness of this form of team organisation. In their review of this report (West and Slater 1996:25) list them as follows :

- Agreed aims, goals and objectives
- Effective communication
- Patients receiving the best possible care
- Individual roles defined and understood.

We may therefore argue that the realisation of these objectives is considered to be essential in realising effective multidisciplinary teamwork settings. One can see how these areas reflect the objectives of multidisciplinarity as linked to teamwork within social/care work practice discussed previously. To this extent recent work within this area does not advocate or identify practices and ways of investigating multidisciplinary practice that are radically different from the literature discussed in the previous section.

Indeed, work within this area (Øvretveit 1997 and Elwyn, Rapport and Kinnersley, 1998) has concentrated on evaluating different models of team-based work and the investigation into the extent to which multidisciplinarity is achieved in practice. Indeed, Elwyn, Rapport and Kinnersley (1998:189) have noted that the existence of a multidisciplinary 'team' in general practice-based primary care is widely questioned echoing the earlier perceptions of Pearson and Van Zwanenberg, (1991). Furthermore, Øvretveit (1997) notes how large teams may result in the emergence of a generalist approach that may hamper the application and facilitation of mutlidisciplinary decision making within team based and other collaborative settings. Why is multidisciplinarity as applied to teamworking problematic? It may well be to do with training, resources and preparation. I do not discount these factors. However, at this stage of the chapter I wish to consider the current way in which multidisciplinarity and team practice are currently thought about and I will argue that this is an important source of the problem.

Respecifying Multidisciplinarity

As noted in earlier sections the linking of multidisciplinarity to team working was discursively achieved through the development of particular conceptualisations of knowledge, communication, interactional structures and roles. Fundamental to both the concept of team and multidisciplinarity are the inter-related concepts of system, structure and function. Lurking within the conceptual foilage of multidisciplinary teamworking is the edifice and influence of structural functionalist thought and notions of a systems-based account of social organisation. Within the realms of social theory considerable time and thought has gone into the debates concerning the Parsonian legacy. However, it is clear that a number of these ideas have proved to be problematic. The approach of Ethnomethodology has sought to respecify some of the most fundamental and treasured ideas of this tradition through the analysis of what people actually do within social settings during the course of their accomplishment. For Garfinkel, a student of Parsons, the notion of the social system had reduced the social actor to the status of 'cultural dope' and the interactional specifics, procedures and methods through which people made sense of and accomplished social organisation was not accounted for. In terms of my research on multidisciplinary teams this provided a starting point for respecifiying multidisciplinary practice through the detailed and rigorous examination of a particular aspect of team practice. The aim here was not to provide a statistically robust evaluation of this form of team practice but to begin to explore the way in which various dimensions of team members practices differed enormously from the theoretical recommendations and commentaries on what multidisciplinary team practice should look like.

However, before exploring the lived detail of multidisciplinary team settings and practices some ethnographic consideration of the team case study explored in this book will be provided. In addition, a consideration of the meeting as an interactional and institutional site will be discussed and identified as a useful site for exploring the accomplishment of team work, whilst acknowledging the existence of other spaces in which team practice and multidisciplinarity can be occasioned.

2 The Multidisciplinary Team, Method and Meetings

Within the conceptual rubric of multidisciplinarity and teamwork, as outlined during the previous chapter, members of a 'multidisciplinary team' are generally described as bringing different modes of expertise to bare on the decision making process of a team working within a community based setting. Thus, a social worker is seen to draw upon a different reservoir of knowledge than an individual who is a trained and practising counsellor. As the previous chapter sought to illustrate this notion is derived from a multidisciplinary focus which suggests that the provision of different modes of expertise oriented toward tackling 'clients needs' generates more holistic and more informed solutions and strategies for professional intervention.

The Multidisciplinary Team Setting Examined

In order to examine some situated aspects of multidisciplinary work and practice within team settings, related and described in this book, I decided to observe the meetings that are regular features of such team-based forms of organisation in social care. In terms of the concept of multidisciplinarity, I considered the observation of meetings an ideal context within which to observe the situated practices of different team members and the situated display of different modes of expertise, roles and opinions. The emphasis on team meetings provided me with a scene within which to examine how the local contingencies and interactional work of a multidisciplinary team was achieved. Furthermore, within such meetings members from different occupational backgrounds and knowledge bases could be observed to be interacting through the arrangement of work, the making of decisions about clients, the exchange of information concerning the task of supporting clients in the community and organisational-work issues arising from team work. Thus, I considered team meetings a suitable focus for this research as they would provide a rich source of data and represented a context within

15

which the team was interactionally realised and work, characterised as multidisciplinary, carried out. In particular, as stated previously, it provided a setting where the display of knowledge, team communication, structure and roles (central to the theoretical models of multidisciplinary practice) could be closely examined. The extent to which interactional work mirrored the descriptions of multidisciplinarity and teamwork discussed during the previous chapter forms one of the considerations of the concluding chapter to this book. *However,* the main focus of this investigation was the praxiological competencies and situated methods through which members of a team accomplished the days work and reflexively constituted the social organisation of the team in and through such interactional activity.

The initial stages of the research involved gaining access to a social work team. This involved producing a letter accounting for my research intentions which was sent to the local social services department and a number of teams in the locality. The letter indicated that I was intending to use recorded 'data' and I made it clear that the anonymity of both speakers and clients would be respected. Furthermore, I also offered the team the opportunity to inspect any of the transcripts that I produced.

I had some limited success, with a number of teams, in terms of written responses to my research request. However, it became clear that some teams wished to exercise a high degree of 'editorial control' over any recorded data that I collected. With respect to the ethnomethodological approach I had adopted this might impair the occasioned nature of any data I might record and transcribe. However, a number of groups indicated an acknowledgement of the potential value of any research into social work at the interactional level. In terms of the parameters of this book the interactional work of a specific multidisciplinary team will be explored. The team focussed upon in this case had been set up in order to provide support of a community that had experienced serious flooding. The organisation of the team was described in terms of a multidisciplinary approach and included a number of team members who were drawn from a variety of professional and non – professional backgrounds.

Having made initial contact with the team I requested that I meet them in order to discuss some of their concerns and answer any questions that they might have regarding my research. This proved to be worthwhile and I was able to establish the necessary trust and communication in order to initiate data collection. Having made the initial preparations I attended both the 'team meetings' and 'allocation meetings' over a period of twelve months. The meetings were held at the beginning of the week and would last between one and two hours. The team meeting consisted of all members of the team and administrative staff and was usually held first. It was followed by the allocation meeting which was attended by qualified social workers and the counsellor. Volunteers and non-social work professionals, other than the counsellor, were not able to attend. The team meeting concerned itself with the agenda for the week, financial matters, the exchange of information, the voicing of members' concerns and a general review of the team's work in relation to the flood hit community and external agencies (for example the local council). Allocation meetings were concerned with the allocation of case work to qualified social workers and often involved discussions about referred clients, their 'needs' and decisions about how best to deal with such referrals. The different categories of meeting and the rules concerning which team members could attend displayed the fact that they were concerned with different and distinct matters. My approach to investigating these phenomena was not distinct. I would simply record the meetings using a compact stereophonic tape recorder that possessed a condensed microphone. In addition to this I would make supplementary notes concerning the position of team members in the room. Having recorded my conversational data, I would transcribe the data utilising a basic form of conversation analytic notation (Jefferson 1984). This notation was able to capture turn taking, interruptions, overlap talk, pauses between utterances and other features of conversational interaction. I then proceeded to analyse the transcribed data utilising a methodological approach that I have described as a reconsidered model of membership categorisation analysis. An approach that I will discuss during the later stages of this chapter.

The Flood Support Team was set up in response to the flooding of a geographical area and nearby town. Furthermore, the adjacent county had experienced serious flooding in previous years; the 'folk memory' was still strong with regard to this event. Both events had been described as 'disasters' and had received widespread and short-lived media attention. The effect on people had been considerable, it had included the loss of property, damage to accommodation, trauma and subsequent financial problems. The effects of flooding had also been seen to produce long term effects that necessitated a response on behalf of the social service departments. A response drafted by the County Social Services Department stated that over 3,500 people had been registered as affected and that some 500 council properties were uninhabited as a consequence of the flooding. The deployment of a specific team with a specific remit of dealing with the 'flood' and its 'victims' was seen as a considered and viable response to the 'needs' of the communities that had been affected. This response noted that if nothing was done problems relating to family breakdown, premature hospital admissions, deterioration of quality of life for poor and elderly people, increase in mental health problems, division, despair and dislocation within communities could result. The response noted that it was politically necessary to act and a proactive stance could be established which would be an effective way of dealing with the problems that the community might suffer.

The Flood Support Team was established with a specific remit. This remit was identified by the response document[1] in the following manner:

The Flood Support Team

Objectives:
To undertake a proactive role in the communities, identifying problems and endeavouring to find solutions
- *To* enable communities to help themselves
- *To* preserve and promote family life
- *To* promote community identity
- *To* enable individuals to retain or regain their place in their communities, especially older people and those with disabilities.

Furthermore, the Flood Support Team drew together professionals and individuals from different agencies. The actual constitution of the Flood Support Team had since its inception, remained constant. The team consisted of the following 'posts' which convey a sense of specific professional identity and 'roles' within the team:

- Clerical Officer
- Volunteer Co-ordinator (seconded from local charity)
- Community Development Worker
- Three Social Workers (with different formal Professional portfolios)
- Counsellor
- Team Leader.

In addition to this, the team had a driver who helped with the delivery/removal of furniture and other transport requirements related to some of the projects that the team sets up. As a consequence the driver was seen as a valuable contributor to the team's work and it was decided democratically by the team members that he should be a formal member of the team organisation.

The specific predicates textually displayed within the Flood Support Team's Report associated with the posts (or role-identities) listed were based on the accepted practices of contemporary personal social service managerial organisation. At a more specific level, these 'posts' were exemplified within some of the reports produced by the Flood Support Team. Each member of the team was described in terms of the activities and tasks they had carried out during the duration of the report. Furthermore, anticipated 'strengths' and 'weaknesses' of specific areas associated with different 'posts' were examined. For example, the community development worker was seen as a member of the team responsible for generating links with the community, sometimes referred to as networks. The developments of such networks might involve liasing with the relevant social service committees, attending local council meetings and developing projects that placed services within community settings. The remit of the 'community development worker' also involved fund raising activities and the publicising of services the team provided within the community. The Flood Support Team Report stated:

> In order that the team to be able to fully integrate its efforts within the communities served, the expertise and knowledge of the community development worker have been great assets. All the projects outlined in this document, with the exception of the furniture service and the stress management group work have developed from work that he has been doing since arriving with the team in late December. Networking with local councillors, voluntary groups and statutory bodies has proved to be beneficial in publicising the remit and scope of the work that we are able to progress.

Thus, whilst the community development worker was not a social worker or a principle provider of care the role predicates of such a post are presented, textually, as of fundamental importance in terms of the teams 'effectiveness' within the discourse of community and community relations.

The post of 'volunteer co-ordinator' is similarly presented within the discursive construction of community. The volunteer co-ordinator is a member of the community who, in this case, had been seconded from a local charitable organisation. The notion of a team member who was seen to be 'of the community' resonates with ideas about what 'community' and, the provision of 'flood support' in the community, entails. The Flood Support Team Report stated:

Volunteers have been a vital part of the practical work that the team has achieved. The furniture service was co-ordinated using almost exclusively volunteers, and many of the projects rely on volunteers and the continuance ... Volunteers have been located for work with individuals and is proving to be a useful service for home care and community care.

In one sense, the representation of volunteers through a volunteer co-ordinator provides for the very stuff of care in the community and the associated notion of empowering communities to 'help themselves'.

A further post is that of the counsellor. The discourse of counselling can be described as both eclectic and highly heterogeneous. The clear representations of counselling as a psychodynamic or cognitive practice is not clearly recognisable in either counselling practice or discourse, however counselling, in a general sense, is concerned with individual psychological states. The Flood Support Team Report did not attempt to clarify such matters. However the counsellor, unlike the community development worker, was statutorily empowered to receive and make referrals due to their position as a qualified social worker practitioner. The counsellor is in the business of providing care and making decisions about clients 'needs'. The Report stated:

The vast majority of referrals are still of women and children with only one man being referred specifically for counselling since August. Although clients are still presenting with stress related symptoms the past few months have shown more clients apathetic and despairing. Although surface of life (e.g. home and immediate community) now look to be back to normal some people feel distressed because their feelings about the disaster are out of parity. It is felt strongly by the Counsellor that many people need permission to feel distressed, although now , almost ten months since the trauma it is normal to have distressing thoughts and feelings.

The provision of counselling within the community is viewed as an important part of flood support. Furthermore, within the description of clients as 'flood victims' the perceived value of counselling 'problems and troubles' of such categorised individuals is high. As has been stated the Flood Support Team consisted of three social workers. Within the remit of the team the provision of social work within the affected communities is seen as a major way of delivering care and the meeting of designated 'needs'. The Flood Support Team Report stated:

The emphasis of the social work effort remains the same, to help and support flood affected families and individuals ... Boundaries for Flood

Support Team intervention have been discussed with each team in the area and the referral of cases between teams progresses and without dispute yet! One social worker, with a background in mental health, works closely with the mental health team, attends their team meetings and is available to that team for emergency duty cover should their needs dictate.

In one sense, the prevailing presentation of social workers as members of a multidisciplinary team is one that involves a degree of movement between agencies and a concern with professional status within a team based setting. This is a description that pertains very much to the previous theoretical accounts of care in the community and multidisciplinary team practice.

Multidisciplinarity and Social Work Team Meetings

The study of multidisciplinary team practice reported in this book is concerned with the examination of the manner in which members achieve multidisciplinarity. Initially, my interest focussed on the notion of how 'theory' was used by members of a team in achieving the locally established assemblage of a multidisciplinary team meeting as practice. In this case, my conceptualisation of theory was concerned with the display of particular collections of knowledge categories (e.g. social theory, management theory and psychological theory). In approaching the topic I did have a preconceived notion of different team members utilising clearly defined and distinct categories of knowledge, which was derived from their professional incumbency (e.g. psychotherapy, community studies and/or managerial science) in a way that was not dissimilar to the theoretical accounts examined in the previous chapter. However, having analysed numerous transcripts gathered from the setting explored it became clear that such a textbook assemblage of multidisciplinarity was simply not in evidence. This was not a setback, rather it enabled me to examine the contingencies of practical action that have been described in some textually organised categorial orders as 'multidisciplinary' and in some of the documents and textual arrangements that the team setting examined in this book produced. Clearly, the assumed gap between idealised textual descriptions, grammars of what multidisciplinary practice (in the form of meetings) might look like and the practical, everyday interactionally achieved reality of such accomplishments would differ in terms of reportage. The approach adopted was not concerned with generating 'idealised types' of action but with documenting naturally occuring conversational interaction within a setting conventionally described as 'multidisciplinary'. Thus, the fundamental concern was to document the practical accomplishment of order in this particular site of interactional work and not as a means of necessarily evaluating the extent to which the locally observed interactional activity 'fitted' some of the notions and generalised ideal types of the textually bound categorial orders outlined earlier.

In adopting this approach in the following chapters, I intend to examine transcripts of recorded conversation from a number of social work meetings. The means through which I will attempt to generate an analysis which illustrates, highlights and draws attention to the concerns above will be through the adoption and utilisation of the reconsidered model of categorisation analysis which will be discussed in the following section of this chapter. As I have previously indicated I will seek to apply the methodological approach to instances of conversational interaction observed and recorded in a number of social work team meetings.

Furthermore, rather than re-constructing formalised schema (i.e. multidisciplinarity and team work as expressed through theoretical discourses) I wish to examine the transcribed data in terms of haecceities of interaction, the 'just thisness', 'right here', methodological work of members practical accomplishment of order. Clearly, team meetings are not solely indicative of 'team work'. They are the fundamental means through which members reflexively orientate themselves interactively to the device 'Flood Support Team', make decisions concerning their work as a team and undertake the overall interactive monitoring and constitution of the team. As stated previously, meetings are a profitable site for enquiry into the interactional accomplishment and display of multidisciplinary teamwork.

As a means of presenting my analysis in this and the following chapters I will seek to examine the data in terms of the following criteria. Firstly, I will seek to examine the conversational and categorial organisation of talk within the team meetings, as a means of illustrating the local social organisation of the conversational interaction within the transcribed data collected. Secondly, I will examine the theoretical notion of 'role' and contrast it to members' interactional work in achieving, utilising, displaying role-identity categories in and through the practical, reflexive, accomplishment of local order. Thirdly, I will seek to examine the interactional display/accomplishment of knowledge within the team meetings examined. I will pursue this, not just as a means of respecifying some of the theoretical accounts discussed earlier in this chapter, but also as a means of illustrating the *ethnomethodological work* in 'communicating' and proffering knowledge and different types of expertise within *in vivo* settings rather than abstracted ideal typical frameworks. Fourthly, I will seek to examine conversational methods which members use in validating claims within the interactional settings observed.

In short, I will seek to respecify some of the professional categorial orders considered in the previous chapter as a means of illustrating the in situ, locally accomplished character of interactional work. It is not my intention to 'disprove' such accounts but merely to concentrate on the business of observing instances of conversational action-in-order within a context that may be textually viewed as fitting a particular model. It is my contention that through the observational analysis of such settings the theoretical accounts of team work, meetings, and multidisciplinarity may be understood not in terms of a categorial order or institutional discourse but in terms of what members actually do in accomplishing such instances of order. Furthermore, I will seek to respecify the rather vague notions of 'functioning' and 'communicating' by illustrating the fine interactional detail of members work within such settings in terms of haeccetic assemblages of observable, recognisable and identifiable members methods for practically accomplishing the task at hand. However, before beginning to outline some basic interactional characteristics of the multidisciplinary team setting in the following chapter and developing these analyses in subsequent chapters, I will provide an outline and description of the methodological approach that informs the commentary, description and analysis that follows.

Analysing Multidisciplinary Settings: The Reconsidered Model of Membership Categorisation Analysis

Within ethnomethodological enquiry, conversation analysis (i.e. the sequential analysis of talk-in-interaction) has been cited as 'the crowning jewel of ethnomethodology' (Button 1991). More recently, debates concerning the relationship between those committed to the sequential analysis of talk and ethnomethodological enquiry have been subject to some debate and small differences of opinion. Many commentators have argued that CA's continued focus upon sequential organisation has led to a situation within which other dimensions of members work within talk (and other activities) has been sidelined with the consequence that an increasingly narrow focus of study is emerging within which the sociological is being underplayed in favour of dialogue with linguistics and notions of interactional social grammar. The purpose of this section is not to pursue this family debate but to explore other precedents within Sacks' work and their development as a means of identifying a complementary ethnomethodological framework for analysing talk-in-interaction, in this case talk and interaction within multidisciplinary team settings.

Membership Categorisation Analysis: Reclaiming Lost Ground

Certain commentators such as Silverman (1998), Hester and Eglin (1997) and Watson (1978) have examined the legacy of Sacks work concerning the development of the methodological approach known as Membership Categorisation Analysis (MCA). As Watson notes, the two approaches of conversation analysis and membership categorisation analysis are not necessarily distinct although in recent years the study of categorisation in talk and interaction has been relegated to the sidelines whilst a concern with sequences in talk has occupied a central position within pragmatic based approaches to the analysis of discourse. Consequently, in recent years the production of MCA studies has begun to establish an arena within which MCA has emerged as a distinct, if not specifically separate, methodological approach.

Sacks' examination of categories and category usage is evident within the large collection of his Lectures' (1992a). One of the most prominent of Sacks' Lectures is concerned with the concept of 'recognisability'. In one sense, this notion refers to the way in which social interactants orient their actions to the mutual task at hand and engage in recognition work as a means of accomplishing local social organisation. This observation, argues Sacks, should inform the examination of interaction as a mutually constitutive, methodical display that is socially recognisable and recognised as part of the process of getting things done in a *social* way rather than a cognitive, economic, theological, biological, telepathic or occult manner. For Sacks, one aspect of this analytical' mentality is a concern with the plethora of description that everyday language exhibits. Furthermore, descriptions occur within a wide range of discursive contexts. For example, newspapers, business meetings and school lessons all provide for the generation of descriptions albeit within different contextual arrangements.

For Sacks, one of the features of conversation and description is the display of categories and the methodical process of categorisation. In Sacks' famous example 'the baby cried the mommy picked it up' these considerations are illuminated by an analytical consideration of how we make sense of the story. In terms of Sacks' example we understand the story in terms of the 'mommy' picking up her 'baby' in response to baby crying. For Sacks, we understand this story in this way because we associate the categories of 'baby' and 'mommy' with the membership categorisation device 'the family'. Of course, both 'baby' and 'mommy' may be categories of further collections such as the 'stage of life device'. However, in order to understand the particular commonsense reading that one usually makes when reading this sentence Sacks invokes two rules of application, namely the economy rule and the consistency rule. The economy rule, according to Sacks (1992,a) refers to the conversational process by which 'if a member uses a single category from any device then he can be recognised to be doing adequate reference to a person'. The following consistency rule states that if a member of a given population has been categorised within a particular device then other members of that population can be categorised in terms of the same collection. Sacks (1992a: 221) derives a corollary known as the hearer's maxim which states:

> If two or more categones are used to categorise two or more members of some population and those categories can be heard as categories from the same collection then: hear them that way.

Sacks used the story, along with the pre-described rules of application, to generate a further set of analytical concepts, namely membership categorisation devices, membership categories and category bound activities. Personal categories such as 'mother', 'father', 'son' or 'daughter' are described by Sacks as membership categories (MC's). Furthermore, they are viewed as membership categories of the membership categorisation device (MCD) 'family'. In addition, this category machinery was complemented by the notion of category bound activities (CBA's) which attempted to describe how certain activities were commonsensically tied to specific categories and devices (e.g. the tying of the activity of crying to the category 'baby'). Sacks' initial ideas of categories or descriptions involved a conceptualisation of an array of 'collections' or a shared 'stock of commonsense knowledge' which membership categorisation devices were seen to encapsulate. For Sacks, therefore, such categorisations and their devices formed part of the commonsensical framework of members' methods and recognisable capacities of practical sense making.

The application of membership categorisation analysis to personal categories and their use by members has been documented (Hester and Eglin 1997, Watson 1978, Jayussi 1984). A seminal piece in the development of membership categorisation analysis is Watson's (1978) paper entitled *'Categorisation, Authorisation and Blame Negotiation in Conversation'* which examines the methodical processes by which members organise descriptions surrounding 'competing claims' and 'competing accounts'. Watson notes how certain membership categories *like* 'punks' and 'hippies', which can be heard to be membership categories of the membership categorisation device 'types of youth subcultures', can become devices in their own right. For example, the membership category 'punk' may also be a device that includes the membership categories of 'bands', 'mohecans' and 'anarchists'. Thus, for Watson the examination of categorisation, authorisation, and blame illustrates how categories can exhibit 'duplicative organisation'. Furthermore, Watson introduces the notion of 'device based properties'. He argues that these predicates feature in the duplicative organisation of categories. For example, the category 'hippy', being a membership category of the device 'types of youth subculture', could be hearably transposed into a device itself through it's mapping on to certain device based properties e.g. smoking marijuana, wearing long hair and ascribing to unorthodox beliefs.

In this paper, Watson also introduces the notions of incumbency with respect to the procedures by which members present themselves in terms of a particular category or identity. The notion of incumbency suggests that identity or role is not a fixed feature of interactants. Rather, identities and role can be understood to be situated interactional achievements and important resources for undertaking various tasks within different settings.

In another early paper entitled *'Accusations: The occasioned use of members knowledge of 'religious geography'*, Drew (1978) examines transcripts from the Scarman Tribunal into Violence and Civil Disorder in Northern Ireland during 1969. Drew draws our attention to how, in the descriptions provided by witnesses, specific geographical place names are used to categorise the religious orientation of 'people involved' and thereby make further inferences on the actions and nature of the events that such persons were seen to be a part. As Drew (1978:3) states:

> An importance of Membership Categories is that they are a conventional basis for ascribing activities (and other characteristics) to persons. Given that a person, group etc., may be characterised in an indefinite number of ways, in someone's activity a speaker may depict that person with that category which is, conventionally, especially relevant to doing that activity.

In many respects, these studies analyse membership categories in terms of personalised configurations and confer the associated predicates to such personalised configurations and, in turn, illustrate the relationship of the associated predicates to such personal collections. However, membership categorisation analysis had also, in some respects, developed from the initial Sacksian concerns with personalised membership category devices into an interest in the use of non-personalised membership categorisation devices in members' talk. For example, McHoul and Watson (1984) examine how commonsense knowledge of the children's own locality is used as a resource in the explanation of formal geographical knowledge. The authors analyse a number of collected transcripts using the three major concepts of MCA; namely membership categorisation devices, membership categories and category bound activities. Thus, during the examination of their transcribed data McHoul and Watson (1984) examine how the term 'public buildings' acts as an MCD, whilst categories such as 'fire station' and 'courthouse' can be understood as membership categories (MC's). The category bound activity or predicate of such categories is described as being 'centrally located' or 'far away' from the City centre. McHoul and Watson note the difficulty of extending MCA, into the territory of non-personalised categories. One of the ways that they seek to deal with the problem of connecting the membership category 'courthouse' with the category bound term 'centrality' is through the consideration of the practice as a 'subject – predicate tie'. Furthermore, this tying of the category with the predicate of 'centrality' is, according to McHoul and Watson, partially resolved (analytically at least) by examining the use of members 'commonsense ecology'. They argue that these two 'axes' are both mutually elaborative and constitutive within their transcribed data.

Further work which has extended the analytic role of MCA into the domain of non personalised categories, as opposed to Sacks' early emphasis with the descriptive categories of person, includes work carried out by Coulter (1983). He seeks to locate categories of social structure within both institutional and organisational conversational contexts as well as every day non-institutional contexts. As Schegloff (1992:102) states with respect to CA's emerging concern with talk and social structure:

> Various aspects of enquiry in this tradition of work have prompted an interest in neighbouring disciplines in relating talk-in-interaction to "contexts" of a more traditional sort – linguistic contexts, cultural contexts, and institutional and social structural contexts. At the same time, investigators working along conversation – analytic lines began to deal with talk with properties which were seemingly related to its production by participants oriented to a "special" institutional context, and, wishing to address those distinctive properties rather than ones held in common

with other forms of talk (as Sacks had done in some of his earliest work based on group-therapy sessions), these investigators faced the analytic problems posed by such an undertaking.

Schegloff continues by stating that such relationships may only be representative of 'discourse-endogenous' terms (e.g. speaker-hearer) and the concern with institutional contexts as merely a form of ethnographic gloss that makes use of transcription resources (e.g. the terms 'doctor' or 'patient' being appended to interlocutors within a specific stretch of talk) as a means of making inferences rather than through the actual data to hand. The problem here is that CA's desire to develop studies in the field of institutional interaction is in a state of tension with its ethno-methodological roots (Hester and Francis, 2001). Namely, a tension between the observable and locally situated character of social organisation that is reflected through a concern with analysing data in terms of what is displayed within the locally produced confines of the talk and the analysts provision of contextual or background information (no matter how small or seemingly insignificant; as in the case of transcribing member category identifications within different forms of formal talk). A further dimension of this context issue is the identification of specialised vocabularies or lexical choice (Levinson, 1997) within formal or institutional settings. It is not at all clear how analysts committed to the rigour of ethno-methodological enquiry can identify,' modes of talk that are identifiable with specialised forms of vocabulary associated with specific professional groups or experts. The strategy of 'externalisation' seems to de-contextualise and ignore the locally produced specifics of members recognition work within 'formal' or 'institutional' settings through the identification of specialised vocabularies *a priori*. A point that will be explored in further detail during the course of this book. At this point, however, it may be noted that the problem of categories and context is one that the extension of membership categorisation analysis into the domain of non-personalised categories provokes. Contemporary developments within MCA have begun to take this problem on board and it is to these developments that I will now turn to.

The Reconsidered Model of Membership Categorisation Analysis

Within recent years the mode of ethnomethodological inquiry known as membership categorisation analysis has been bolstered by a series of studies which have sought to take on board many of the issues discussed above. This has led to a development of an analytical mentality which is sensitive to context, the relationship between sequentiality and category work and the local production of social order (Watson 1997). In order to explicate this further, a consideration of recent work on categories in context will now be undertaken.

Categories in Context

The notion of membership categorisation analysis providing a componential framework for language use is taken up by Hester in a paper entitled '*Categories in Context*' (1994). Hester argues that Sacks' work involves an ambiguous approach to membership categories and their analysis. According to Hester such ambiguity was expressed through the development of two models or concerns, namely the '*de-contextualised model*' and the '*occasioned mode*'. The de-contextualised model is seen to be an interpretation of MCA in a way not dissimilar to the work of Noam Chomsky's theory of transformational grammar and the school of cognitive anthropology. As Hester (1994:221) states:

> Such a decontextualised approach is exemplified in the work of Cognitive Anthropology and in the work of Chomsky on transformational generative grammar, both of which seek to provide formal accounts of a determinate structure of knowledge which members or speaker-hearers are said to possess for producing meaningful descriptions as a precondition for competent interaction.

For Hester, such an interpretation of MCA negates the potential reading of the MCA methodological framework as one which pays attention to the local use of categories by members 'in situ', i.e. categorisation and the use of categories as an occasioned phenomenon. Hester argues for a reconsideration of the use of categories by members in the contextual settings of their production. Furthermore, the notion of context advanced does not merely refer to the parameters of social interaction but to context as an indexical and reflexive accomplishment by members. Therefore, the term 'categories in context' refers to a display of categories in different contexts that can be understood as a mutually constitutive interactional achievement of members' practical linguistic work. This is quite distinct from a restraining view of context as an unspoken reified parameter that informs or influences the interactional display of categories in conversation, *context is not imposed, it is achieved.* Indeed, the use of categories in talk is viewed as a locally achieved phenomenon. Insofar as they are situated phenomena which are made recognisable by the methodical procedures of members' interactional activity. Thus, the occasioned model of MCA would be one which focuses on such considerations by illustrating the local production of interaction as an endogenous reflexive accomplishment.

Consequently, a framework for MCA as a methodological approach which eschews the analytical location of categories within specific, stable culturally defined collections is made possible. As Hester notes, the irremediable indexical meaning of words lie in their use, and not in any general use, but their specific display within localised practical interactional achievements. As Hester (1994:242) argues:

> Membership categorisation devices or collections are therefore to be regarded as in situ achievements of members' practical actions and practical reasoning. Categories are 'collected' with others in the course of their being used. In turn, then, this means that the 'collection' to which a category belongs is constituted through its use in a particular context; it is part and parcel of its use in that way. Its recognisability is part of the phenomena itself. What 'collection' the category belong to, and what the collection is, are constituted in and how it is used this time.

In many respects Watson's notion of 'duplicative organisation' (i.e. the possibility of membership categories becoming or being heard as membership categorisation devices) complements the notions of context and the haeccetic production and deployment of categories in context. Furthermore, the eschewing of stable, culturally defined collections of categories and the view of collections being locally produced phenomena allows for a more thorough analysis of both personal modes of categorisation and non-personal modes of categorisation deployed by members in conversation. This process is also enhanced by the transposition of the notion of category bound activities into a more contextually and locally sensitive concern with predicates. Predication is not necessarily seen to be bound up with a specific category as such but refers to the type of associations, activities and attributes that might be imputed or mapped onto a particular category or device. This transposition provides for the associated ideas of *conversationally tied predicates and occasioned collections*. This notion provides for the way in which members' category work may build up modes of categorisation through the topic and conversational materials at hand and as they are produced by members in situ. Thus, the notion of 'natural collections', and the notion of stable external bodies of clearly identifiable commonsense collections, is eschewed in favour of a sensitivity to the *in situ* and locally occasioned character of members' category work. This also allows for a consideration of the way in which members tie predicates to devices and categories in terms of the practicality of such connections and the particular here and now activities oriented to in-talk.

Categories and the Sequential Organisation of Conversation

The development of conversation analysis and membership categorisation analysis as two distinct ethnomethodological analytical approaches to language activities has been documented. For example, conversation analysis is seen to be concerned with the *sequential organisation of conversation* whilst categorisation analysis is seen to be concerned with the methods of *categorisation and the display of categories and their associated predicates* in both naturally occurring talk and textual formations'. However, recalling Sacks' famous story 'The baby cried, the mommy picked it up' the introduction to notions of membership categories and collections the practice of making sense of such categorisations (i.e. Sacks's 'rules of application') is implicitly tied to sequential organisation. The order within which the categories flow is of crucial importance to the sense of the utterance. For example, in the case of the consistency rule, Sacks (1992a: 239) states:

> Now one basic rule in the use of these things, I'll call the 'consistency rule'. It holds that if you are categorising some population of persons − if a member is categorising some population of persons − then if they've used one category from some collection for the *first* (*my* emphasis) person they're going to categorise, they may − it is legitimate, permissible to categorise the rest of the population by the use of the same or other categories of the same population by the use of the same categories or other categories of the same population.

Whilst Sacks, in this early discussion surrounding membership categorisation analysis, merely hints at questions surrounding categories and sequentiality it is clearly a potential reading which is at the heart of Sacks early work. Within the reconsidered model of Categorisation Analysis as developed by Hester and Eglin (1997), Housley and Fitzgerald (2002) and the authoritative work of Watson (1978,1997) questions surrounding sequentiality and categorisation work have been mooted and discussed. However, as yet, no definitive publication has provided a considered analysis, although the work of Hester and Eglin (1997) represents a collection of studies and discussions that help to remedy this situation. Within this collection, Watson (1997:54) claims that the relationship between categorisation and sequentiality in conversation can be explained in the following terms:

> What I am claiming ... is that interlocutors' sensible production and monitoring of an utterance and of a series of utterances is both categorical and sequential. Interlocutors' conjoint orientation to categorial relevancies informs their orientation to the 'structure' of utterance and series which in turn inform the categorial relevancies. In Aaron Cicourel's apt phrase, there is a 'folding back effect' on the utterance production and monitoring, a darting back and forth reflexive consultation of categorial and sequential relevances in order that utterance or series be rendered describable or identifiable as transacting this or that activity, as forming a component of this or that overall course of action and social setting.

Watson's notion of 'reflexive monitoring' reminds us of Garfinkel's concept of the documentary method of interpretation in the sense that the sequential positioning and categorial organisation of utterances provide resources for the search for underlying patterns in accounting for various forms and displays within talk-in-interaction. It is through this praxiological orientation that the 'normal form' of conversational interaction, i.e. the methods for producing a sense of order, involve methods in which sequence and categorisation are contextually embedded features through which such local instances of order are achieved. This reflexive process can also be understood in terms of the manner through which categories are sequentially managed, configured, arranged and displayed. This management of categories in talk is a reflexive process in that the task at hand (e.g. the activity of explaining) consists of an interactive mutually constitutive process of category display and sequential organisation/management. Therefore, as Silverman (1998:152) notes both category and sequence can be understood 'to be two sides of the same coin'.

Categories and Normative Order

A further dimension of the reconsidered model of membership categorisation analysis is the normative principles and practice of categorisation. Clearly in terms of population groups categorisation can often be articulated within easily identifiable parameters of normativity. However, non-personal objects and their categorisation clearly display a normative organisation in the sense that utterances often not only derive their sense from 'stocks of common sense knowledge' but can also, in terms of categories in context, be mapped and tied to other categories in terms of locally situated conditions of relevance, activity and context. Thus normativity, or norms in action, are applied in a variety of different ways within occasioned circumstances. Jayussi (1991) has investigated the moral organisation of categorisation in considerable depth. For Jayussi, Sacks' work on membership categorisation and subsequent studies (Drew, 1978, Coulter 1979, Sharrock 1974, Pomerantz 1978 and Watson 1983) have identified and explicated the moral inferential logic (Jayussi 1991:240) of everyday social practice. Jayussi (1991:240) states:

> Sacks' notion of category bound actions, rights and obligations not only points out the moral features of our category concepts, but also provides thus for the very moral accountability of certain actions of omissions. His elucidation of the notion of certain categories as standardised relational pairs ... not only uncovers features of the organisation of members' conventional knowledge of the social world, but clearly demonstrates via empirical analysis, how that knowledge is both morally constituted and constitutive of moral praxis − it provides for a variety of ascriptions, discoveries, imputations, conclusions, judgements etc. on the part of mundane reasoners.

Thus, echoing Wittgenstein later work Jayussi notes how ethnomethodological analysis has illustrated how practical activities (e.g. asking questions, providing descriptions and making 'sense') are also inexorably moral. Jayussi (1991:241) continues by stating:

> I have elsewhere, building on Sacks' work, tried to show in some detail how moral reasoning is practically organised, and how, at the same time, and perhaps more significantly, practical reasoning is morally organised ... Very clearly, the use of even mundanely descriptive categories, such as 'mother', 'doctor', 'policeman', for example, makes available a variety of possible inferential trajectories *in situ,* that are grounded in the various 'features' bound up with, or constitutive of, these categories as organisations of practical mundane social knowledge. These features might be 'moral' features in the first place (such as the kinds of 'rights' and 'obligations' that are bound up with one's being a 'mother', or a 'doctor' or 'policeman'), or they might be otherwise − such as the 'knowledge' that is for example, taken to be bound up with a category such as 'doctor', or the kind of 'work' that is taken to be constitutive of, or tied to, a category such as a policeman. But even in the latter case, it turns out that as evidenced in our actual practices, for example,

'knowledge' has its responsibilities — even these features provide grounds for the attribution of all kinds of moral properties, for finding that certain kinds of events or actions may or may not have taken place, for determining culpability, even for defeating the applicability of the category or description in the first place.

Thus, Jayussi illustrates and defines the mutually constitutive and reflexive relationship between practical action and normativity. Furthermore, the process of categorisation in both it's personal and non-personal forms can be understood to be moral in character. Pomerantz notes how preference organisation within adjacency pair formats identified by more sequential analyses of talk-in-interaction can also be understood in terms of practical-moral inferential work. However, the reconsidered model of membership categorisation analysis aims to incorporate a concern for categorisation and sequential work in talk-in-interaction. Indeed, the fulfilment of a second part within an adjacency pair is not just a sequential phenomenon. In terms of recipient design we can note how categorial design is central to the smooth fulfilment of the second part. The reciprocity of perspective and the Garfinklian notion of trust (a necessary lubricant for all interaction as Garfinkels' breaching experiments illustrated) is one within which the moral-practical work of categorisation and sequential organisation forms an important part.

Categories and Social Structure

The relationship between the 'micro' concerns of ethnomethodological forms of enquiry and wider 'macro' approaches is one fraught with misunderstanding and misinterpretation. Not least because many ethnomethodological forms of enquiry do not recognise this form of sociological dualism. However, in recent years the relationship between wider social structure and ethnomethodological concerns with the situated production and accomplishment of social organisation has been entertained. One of the more notable discussions concerning this relationship is provided by Boden and Zimmerman (1991) who note how senses and configurations of social structure (e.g. class, race and gender) are interactionally accomplished *in situ*. In many ways, the reconsidered model of membership categorisation analysis facilitates this idea by drawing attention to how local configurations of categorisation may also involve a recognisable appeal to wider social process, concerns and factors as part and parcel of the inferential work of members everyday affairs. Thus, in the case of national identity, which some sociologists have conceived of as socially constructed and imagined (Fevre and Thompson, 1999) membership categorisation analysis has illustrated the manner through which senses of 'national' identity are in fact local configurations of social organisation that provide resources for particular types of activity e.g. prejudice, inferring 'underlying' characteristics and locating opinions (Hester and Housley, 2001).

A further dimension of this set of local practices is elegantly outlined by Hester and Eglin (1997) who note how Sacks notion of membership categorisation included a notion of culture as an 'inference making machine'. Clearly, the practice of making inferences is not just a process of accounting for observations in relation to a static body or set of cultural knowledge deposited and internalised by members through a process of primary and secondary socialisation. On the contrary, inference making, in the sense that Sacks employs it, provides for the *local* social organisation of facts, observations and relevance's of a particular set of conditions and predicated inferences. The cultural inference machine becomes, therefore, an instance and manifestation of culture-in-action rather than culture as a cultural backdrop upon which social action is constituted and realised. Consequently, within the framework of the new synthesis within sociological enquiry and the drive to overcome dualism (Tucker, 1998) the reconsidered model of membership categorisation analysis provides an interesting way of analysing and documenting how members' senses of wider social structure and culture impinge upon everyday social interaction.

During this section of the chapter I have explored a specific form of ethnomethodological analysis that seeks to analyse talk and interaction in a manner that incorporates a range of interactional specifics, details and concerns that is not reduced merely to the level of sequential organisation (though this is a very important dimension of the local organisation of social interaction). In the following chapter I will begin to apply some concerns of the reconsidered model of MCA to some basic practices observed within multidisciplinary meetings. I will then develop this foundational analyses and begin to explore a range of topics in the following chapters that are tied to issues surrounding models of multidisciplinary team practice. However, before initiating this focus on analysis I wish to develop the previous discussion of meetings as methodologically interesting sites and settings. I wish to do this as a means of focussing upon the site prior to analysis and observation and in order to make some further connection with debates and issues surrounding 'institutional interaction' that are of relevance to many of the points and observations made during the course of the following chapters and the book as a whole. In this sense the book can be read as one that is relevant to our understanding of interaction in multidisciplinary teams and as a methodological commentary on interaction in formal and institutional settings.

The Meeting as an Interactional and Institutional Site

The convention of the meeting is one that is so old, that its origins are perhaps as obscure as the appearance of language amongst our species. It is a primordial activity that has been used as a means of getting a number of social activities done. These activities often involve an exchange of information and an orientation to decision making. The use of the meeting as an organisational device is not an object of management science, it is a device that members of society use during the course of their everyday lives. However, this lay device has become increasingly 'institutionalised' and various models of 'meetings' have been devised and propagated as a means of 'increasing effectiveness' within organisations. However, ethnomethodological studies of meetings have examined them in terms of a particular set of activities and conversational interaction. For example, Hester's work on referral talk (1992) examines the actions and practices carried out in describing pupils as exhibiting 'problems or needs' within referral meetings between teachers and educational psychologists. For Hester, the meeting is a practically constituted and locally produced set of activities and accomplishments that constitutes a particular interactional order. Thus, we may conceive of meetings as particular types of devices that various predicates, e.g. sharing information, making referrals, making decisions etc, can be tied.

The examination of communication, information exchange, understanding and dialogue within multidisciplinary teams has been described in terms of a number of different processes. However, in the examination of multidisciplinary team meetings presented in this book, the conversational activities of teams within meetings is viewed as the main way through which members carry out and realise teamwork. Clearly, the team meeting is not the only expression of multidisciplinary team work, however it is representative of a fundamental expression of teamwork and, according to the theoretical models explored in chapter one, multidisciplinary practice. Indeed, in many respects meetings are the primary ways in which a sense of teamwork is realised. Consequently, the examination of the decision making process (and the way in which different modes of expertise inform such a process) will be examined in terms of conversational interaction. Written reports, documents and issues surrounding professional practice and confidentiality are important, however I wish to focus on the domain that Øvretveit (1987) describes as dialogue, meaning and the exchange of information and relate these in the course of the book to issues surrounding team roles, knowledge display and the reflexively tied domain of team narrative and localised rhetorics.

The focussed examination of conversational interaction within meetings remains relatively unexplored, although many commentators and analysts have explored institutional sites and activities within which meeting type talk may occur. In addition to Hester's work (1992), we may add the work of Ramcharan (1993) Francis (1992) and Payne (1978) that are notable exceptions to this point. It would seem that an examination of conversational interaction is of fundamental importance to understanding the dimensions and lived reality of communicating within teams and making decisions about clients 'needs'. The abstract theoretical accounts of multidisciplinary social work practice are heavily grounded within the systemic accounts of team organisation and function. Such accounts, from an ethnomethodological point of view, compound traditional sociological enquiries orientation towards operationalising theorised accounts of the social in explaining societal processes and informing policies and initiatives through a varied range of recommendations and general observations. One strand of conversation analytic enquiry, which has examined professional practice and interaction, is known as the Institutional Talk Program. The aims of this programme can be said to involve a concern with documenting and examining the particular properties of formal talk within institutional contexts (e.g. clinics, hospitals, courtrooms and meetings). This approach towards the examination of talk that displays 'institutionality' can be understood to include multidisciplinary team talk. As Hester and Francis (2002:2) put it:

> The basic assumption of the Institutional Talk Programme (hereafter ITP) is that the concepts and methods of CA can be extended beyond the study of 'ordinary conversation' to the investigation of various forms of 'institutional talk' in order to show that such interaction differs from ordinary conversation *in systematic ways*. Where CA has focussed upon the organisation of ordinary conversation, ITP aims to describe the organisation of 'institutional talk and interaction'. At the heart of ITP studies is the claim that that the sequential organisational characteristics of 'ordinary conversation' comprise a 'bedrock' to which other 'speech exchange systems' are tied as specific modifications of that 'paramount system'.

During the course of our consideration of multidisciplinary team talk its is useful to explore this approach that has informed discursive and conversation analytic studies of the workplace. It is to a wider consideration of this approach that we now turn.

The Institutional Talk Program

The display of categories and conversational sequences within institutional settings is well documented within ethnomethodological and interactionist based studies. In a book entitled *Talk at Work: Interaction in institutional settings* (Drew and Heritage 1992), a collection of discourse analytic and conversation analytic studies provide a contemporary corpus of material that is concerned with linguistic discourse in the work place and professional contexts. The opening three chapters of this dense collection involves a consideration of the theoretical and analytical issues involved in studying the conversational characteristics of institutional discourse.

Drew and Heritage begin with an acceptance that there is not 'necessarily a hard and fast distinction between 'ordinary conversation' and 'institutional conversation'. Furthermore, they describe their task as one that does not correspond to the construction of a concrete definition of institutional 'talk'; rather their interest is said to lie in the development of an analytic concern for identifying 'features that may contribute to family resemblance's among cases of institutional talk that are predominantly addressed in the chapters that follow' (1992:21).

For Drew and Heritage, a concern for the contextual specifics of institutional talk is well served by the conversation analytic framework proffered by Emmanuel Schegloff (1973). Conversation analysis provides a wide corpus of work which also provides for a comparative approach whilst paying attention to the detail of in situ locally produced contexts. In analysing institutional talk, the observation made by Schegloff in chapter three of the collection, is referred to as a useful methodological consideration. This consideration asserts that whilst an 'intuitive' connection between social interaction and social structure can be heard (e.g. references to ethnicity or status), the temptation to provide 'factual correctness' should be avoided and the spectre of positivism deflected via the acknowledgement that a number of readings of interactional data is possible. Placing themselves within the context of Schegloff's recommendation, Drew and Heritage (1992:20) argue that the studies contained in the volume,

... are concerned to show that analytically relevant characterisations of social interactants are grounded in empirical observations that show that the participants themselves are demonstrably orientated to the identities or attributes in question.

Having established their analytical orientation Drew and Heritage (1992:22) continue by focussing on some features of institutional talk gleaned from the studies included in their collection. The following propositions are made:

1   Institutional interaction involves an orientation by at least one of the participants to some core goal, task or identity (or set of them) conventionally associated with the institution in question. In short, institutional talk is normally informed by goal orientations of a relatively restricted conventional form.

2   Institutional interaction may often involve special and particular constraints on what one or both of the participants will treat as allowable contributions to the business at hand.

3   Institutional talk may be associated with inferential frameworks and procedures that are particular to specific institutional contexts.

Drew and Heritage develop these proposals by referring to specific analytic concerns involved in examining institutional contexts. Following the work of Sacks, Schegloff and Jefferson (1974) on interaction in Courtrooms, Mehan (1978) in classrooms and Greatbatch (1988) on news interviews, the notion that institutional talk exhibits formal conversational procedures and methods is advanced. These procedures and methods may involve specific displays of specialised vocabulary, or as Levinson (1995) phrases it 'lexical choice'. For those interested in advancing the remit of ITP the examination of lexical choice is a further way through which institutionality, via the display of professional, technical or lay vocabularies, can be explored. Furthermore, specific formal forms of turn design may be observed, these formal forms of turn design reflect the famous 'I.R.E.' structure discussed by Mehan (1978) and others in ethnomethodological studies of formal classroom talk. The sequential organisation of topic and the overall 'structural organisation' of talk in institutional contexts is also seen as an area where formal properties of members talk may be observed. To this extent ordinary conversation is contrasted with various properties of institutional discourse. As Heritage (1985:6) argues:

...Mundane Conversation − [is]... the primary and prototypical form of language usage − ... the fundamental 'baseline' from which various forms of institutional interaction depart.

An additional concept that Drew and Heritage provide in their analytic resume of the Institutional Talk program is that of 'interactional asymmetries in institutional settings'. The notion refers to the distinction between ordinary conversation, within which it is alleged interlocuters are orientated towards equal speaking rights, whilst formal/institutional conversation is oriented to the display of asymmetrical conversational modalities. This asymmetry is summarised by work carried out by Heritage and Greatbatch (1993:95) who state:

> The studies which have reported these findings have been influential for two reasons. First, turn taking organisations − whether for conversation or institutional contexts such as courtroom interaction − are a fundamental and generic aspect of the organisation of interaction. They are organisations whose features are implemented recurrently over the course of interactional events. This characteristic gives them a special methodological interest for students of institutional talk. For if it can be shown that the participants in a vernacularly characterised institutional setting such as a courtroom pervasively organise their turn taking in a way that is distinctive from ordinary conversation, it can be proposed that they are organising their conduct so as to display and realise its 'institutional' character over its course and that they are doing so recurrently and pervasively.

However, Drew and Heritage attempt to emphasise the local in situ nature of such asymmetry whilst recognising that some researchers (e.g. Blumstein and Schwartz 1985) have an interest in relating such local, endogenous manifestations to wider social structural issues of status and power.

A further analytical category included in this overview is one described as 'social epistemology'. This refers to modes of interactional work that situate formal talk in relation to specific co-participants. For example, a doctor may display 'professional cautiousness' in talking to patients. Heritage and Drew view such procedures in terms of what Whalen and Zimmerman (1990) describe as practical epistemological work. In other words, situating and interactionally constituting the elicitation of knowledge in terms of the local contextually bound 'reality' at hand. The approach adopted by the institutional talk program has been criticised by certain ethnomethodologically oriented commentators. Whilst Schegloff (1992) urges a cautious approach to the construction of a formalised model of institutional talk, Hester and Francis (forthcoming) have taken a more critical stance to the institutional talk program (henceforth referred to as ITP). The main thrust of the criticism centres around the notion that ITP *despite its good intentions* relegates the in situ interactional accomplishment of context by members via here and now interactional, conversational methods and activities. Consequently, the criticisms can be understood to be primarily methodological. The desire to construct pre-formalised analytical tools (as listed above) can be discerned in the ITP's observations and produce what Hester and Eglin describe as 'motivated explanations'. For example, Drew and Heritage (1992:31) with reference to a stretch of talk gathered during a study conducted by Silverman (1987, ch.3) that deals with the interaction between a doctor and a mother in a paediatric clinic, state:

> These observations, in turn, open up a rich vein of analysis which can focus on the use of *we* and *I* by incumbents of institutional roles (see Maynard 1984; Silverman 1987; West 1990); for example, in the following a doctor is recommending a test to the parents of a child with a heart condition:
>
> (4) [Silverman 1987:58]
> 1. Dr: Hm (2.0) the the reason for doing the test
> 2.   -> is , I mean I'm 99 per cent certain that all she's got is a
> 3. ductus
> 4. F: Hm Hm
> 5. M: I see
> 6. Dr:-> However the time to find out that we're
> 7.   wrong is not when she's on the operating
> 8.   table.

Here the switch from *I* to *We* is significant not merely as a shift from a more to a less "democratic" referring expression (Silverman 1987), but also as a means for the doctor to avoid saying *the time to find out when I'm wrong is not* ...which would overtly raise the possibility of his being personally responsible for a clinical error.

For Hester and Francis (2001:12), such a reading represents 'the activity of imputing specific motivations to participants on the basis of an analyst's version of categorically defined interests results in an even more tendentious account of the data'. For Hester and Francis, the use of the term 'we' can be explained via a number of different explanations. For example, they argue that the use of the term 'we' could be seen to represent a method of displaying collaboration between the patient's parent and the doctor. Alternatively, the pro-term could also be heard to refer to a medical team who are responsible for making decisions and carrying out operations on young children. This is a view that is also echoed by Watson (1997), who argues that the conventions of providing a notational device for who is speaking within transcribed data (e.g. doctor or psychiatrist) are used as an analysts resource for inferring relationships between role and professional identity and the displayed talk. Watson argues that it is for the incumbents to make relevant the incumbent nature of their talk *rather than the analyst.*

For Hester and Francis, such motivated readings ignore the issue of context as an interactionally achieved phenomenon. Hester and Francis (1997:17) state:

> The recognisability of any stretch of interaction as, say, a medical consultation, a news interview or a classroom lesson is not to be found in any formal properties of the talk in and through which these activities are conducted. Such recognisability is a situated accomplishment, and involves a reflexive relationship between utterances, situated identities and other circumstantial particulars.

Having discussed some of the problems of ITP, I would like to point out that such problems are methodological ones rather than serious analytical fractures. It is clear that some of the ideas developed within ITP are relevant to the study of multidisciplinarity and team discourse, in the sense that they can be construed as both formal and institutional sites of local, discursive production. However, the criticisms of ITP also have to be imbibed. The fundamental criticism, i.e. the lack of concern for the local in situ production of order and context, is one that fires the ethnomethodological concern with *members' methods* rather than *analysts formalisations.* Having discussed some of the general methodological concerns of more formal institutional analyses, whilst not rejecting such analyses as incorrect, I have examined the transcriptions of the meetings that I observed in terms of the reconsidered model of membership categorisation analysis discussed during the course of this chapter. Such a reconsidered analytical approach is, it has been argued, sensitive to the local production of orderly activities and the interactional realisation of context as a here and now activity. Whilst Drew and Heritage are aware of both the bucket theory of context and the ethnomethodological approach to context, other commentators see ITP as somewhat relaxed in implementing such concerns analytically. However, it is the relegation of local *in situ* concerns to institutional parameters within the ITP programme that is of concern to those interested in studies of situated action. The need to adhere to the notion that context is achieved and not imposed is of paramount importance to those interested in investigating ethnomethodological phenomenon. In the last analysis, we may recall Garfinkel's call to move from a notion of quiddity (the 'missing' interactional 'what' of achieved assemblages of order and practices) to haecceity (i.e. the just 'thisness' of members' praxiological accomplishments). In one sense, the concern of ITP to document, illustrate and identify methods and molecular conversational structures that are representative of something called 'Institutional Talk' is to remain tied to notions of a 'missing what' of specific species of order, discipline or set of 'core practices' within specific institutional settings. However, this orientation to illuminating the missing interactional what of 'institutional interaction' or 'laboratory work' (i.e. the haecceity of these settings) can according to Lynch (1993:276):

> ... encourage misunderstandings of what ethnomethodological studies might be about. References to a 'missing what' and 'unique adequacy' encourage a conception of each disciplinary speciality as a unique species of practice defined by a singular essence that can be comprehended only by 'getting inside' the relevant epistemic circle.

Thus, whilst it may be argued that the examination of 'institutional talk' may not be seen as a separate discipline, the notion of institutional talk can be seen to refer to a particular species of conversational interaction that is not particular to local circumstances but to a specific collection of locations and 'contextual backdrops'. It is within these settings that ITP claims common conversational structures and methods can be observed. To this extent, the haecceity of conversational interaction, the *in situ*, ad hoc, local accomplishment of order is relegated in a push to provide a formalised schema for a molecular sociology of social institutions. However, this is a move that ethnomethodology has shown to be highly problematic and divorced from the locally produced, in vivo, members' accomplishment of interactional order.

During the following chapter I will attempt to begin to respecify multidisciplinary team practice through a basic examination of the interactional contours of teamwork in settings traditionally described as 'meetings'. Indeed, these are often the only sites where teams are able to assemble and accomplish a sense of 'team-ness'. It may well be the case that meetings, as sites of institutionality, are examples of an enunciative modality from and through which institutional discourse is both produced and is reproduced. However, I wish to take on board some of the observations of automatically treating talk-in-interaction in formal settings (in this case within multidisciplinary team meetings) as 'institutional'. Rather, the focus will be firmly on how notions of team, and other formal properties or notions are accomplished by members. The notion of interaction taking place within the frame of institutional parameters can inform and yield important insights, however, it may also serve to gloss over the situated character of members practices in settings that may lend themselves to such a description.

Note

1   The response document is not reproduced here due to matters of confidentiality.

3 Respecifying Multidisciplinary Social Work Meetings

A respecification of multidisciplinary social work practice within settings described as meetings requires an examination of conversational interaction in terms of the methodological framework discussed in the previous chapter. Furthermore, it necessitates an examination of naturally occurring, conversational interaction within relevantly achieved social contexts. The examination of conversational interaction is, in one sense, representative of the linguistic turn within sociology. It is an acknowledgement of the way in which concepts such as exchanging information, communicating and meaning are primarily discursive phenomena. The structural account of processes within system based models of team work represent a mode of theorising which 'misses the interactional what' of the phenomena that it seeks to describe. Furthermore, within the field of multidisciplinary teamwork the interactional and conversational dimensions of teamwork demand examination. However, in order to initiate the examination of the linguistic and interactional credentials and characteristics of teamwork I will begin this chapter by making some basic observations about the interactional organisation of team meeting settings. Consequently, I do not want to address the meeting as an institutional structure or parameter within which conversational interaction takes place. For to do so would be to implicitly accept the notion that talk-in-meetings is informed or shaped by such a configuration; rather than viewing such interactional orders as endogenous, situated accomplishments. However, in order to examine the way in which such accomplishments, tasks and senses of order are achieved I wish to apply the principles of a reconsidered model of MCA to the analysis of talk recorded and represented in the transcribed data. This will, initially, involve a concern with category and sequence in team members talk-in-interaction. However, in later stages of this book I will develop analyses of multidisciplinary team meeting talk that encompass the various dimensions of this form of analysis (as it relates to specific cases and practices) outlined in the previous chapter.

The Local Management of Categories

With respect to the issues surrounding the relationship between conversation analysis and membership categorisation analysis discussed in terms of the reconsidered model of MCA, I should like to introduce the notion of i.) category display and ii.) the sequential management of categories-in-talk. Category display refers to the use and deployment, by members, of categories in talk. Furthermore, this notion is grounded in the praxiology of membership categorisation devices, membership categories, modes of predication and the associated rules of application. Thus, category display refers to those methods of categorisation that are made recognisable in and through conversational interaction and the local, practical accomplishment of order. The concern with 'display' is an attempt to draw attention to the way in which categories are made recognisable (in and through talk) and how this activity is a fundamental feature of talk-in-interaction. However, in attempting to address the relationship between categories in talk and sequentiality I seek to propose that, as Harvey Sacks (1972) initially noted, that categories are sequentially organised in and through observable structures. These observable structures can be understood as the means through which members manage categories in talk. Furthermore, as has been previously noted, categories and sequence are reflexively and mutually constitutive. Watson (1997) notes that Schegloff and Sacks formulation of adjacency pairs did not, initially, characterise the categorial relationship between, for example, a question and a proffered answer. Watson begins to note the way in which recipiency, as a sequential phenomena, can also be thought to involve category work, which through specific procedural work such as the consistency rule, can be understood to be exhibiting a 'tying procedure' that may establish '... the specific relatedness of just this answer to just this question, here and now' (Watson 1997: 59). Thus, the analogy is not a strict demarcation, but is a useful analytical distinction in illustrating the conversational, social and praxiological organisation of the meeting talk that will be examined. I will begin by focussing on the sequential methods for managing talk before attempting to consider how such management of talk, as Watson has suggested, is related to the categories displayed within talk-in-interaction. This will provide for an examination of the conversational work within meetings and prepare the ground for the consideration of further analyses of multidisciplinary teamwork and organisation within the context of the meeting talk observed, documented and discussed in the course of this book.

Identifying Categorial and Sequential Methods within Meetings

Within traditional modes of sociological inquiry the social organisation of a meeting may be equated with notions of social structure and the experience of social actors in terms of such structural components and the attendant processes of power, labelling and social control. However, in ethnomethodological terms the social organisation of meetings and other similar social activities have been observed to consist of members practical work displayed through conversational interaction (Hester and Francis 1996). Consequently, whilst other resources may be used by members (such as seating arrangements and the local geography of the space in which such activities are to be carried out) the language activities of members is axiomatic to the process of doing a meeting. As has been stated, from an ethnomethodological point of view, a view established through observational studies, the social organisation of meetings necessitates an examination of the social organisation of talk. This social organisation of talk, according to ethnomethodology, can be examined through the observation of the conversational methods that members use in constituting the activity of a meeting. It is to these methods, as displayed by members in the team meetings examined, that we now turn.

Some Basic Conversational Machinery for Doing Meetings

Turn Taking

The structure of conversation has been of prime importance to conversation analysis and categorisation analysis. The seminal paper by Sacks, Schegloff and Jefferson (1974) presents the method of 'turn taking' as the basic sequential unit of conversation. Furthermore, Sacks draws our attention to the notion of 'adjacency pairs' which, according to Coulthard (1977:70), possess the following characteristics:

> ...they are two sentences long; the utterances are produced successively by different speakers, the utterances are ordered – the first must belong to the class of first pair parts, the second to the class of second pair parts; the utterances are related, not any second pair can follow any first pair, but only an appropriate; the first pair part often selects next speaker and always selects next action – it thus sets a transition relevance and expectation which the next speaker fulfils, in other words the first part of the pair predicts the occurrence of the second. (1977:70)

The 'discovery' of structural units within conversational interaction heralded the drive towards the sequential analysis of conversation. For Sacks, turn taking was representative of those 'naturally occurring social activities' which he believed could be submitted to formal investigations. Consequently, Sacks argued that sociology could be a primitive observational science that examined the 'formal procedures which members employ'. Schegloff's seminal studies on turn taking (1968,1979) yielded a number of important observations. However, it is the way in which adjacency pairs exhibit what Sacks calls recipient design[1] that is of considerable interest in any consideration of turn-taking. For example, adjacency pairs may take the form of a question and answer sequence or complaint and apology sequence. As has been noted in chapter two, Sacks et al (1974) draw our attention to different turn taking systems, for example in 'formal' or 'institutional' contexts turns may be 'pre-allocated', as in teacher-pupil interaction, in which overlaps and interruptions are minimised. The principles of adjacency and recipient design still hold within formal turn taking systems such as the IRE speech exchange mechanism. Within pedagogical discourse, each component describes particular predicated forms of design. In other words, the design is not spontaneous but is organised in order to fulfil local contingencies of conversational order and social interaction.

From an ethnomethodological point of view, the examination of the mundane was seen as a way of illustrating the lived orderliness of social life. The significance of turn taking structures was, according to Psathas (1995:17), that:

> Order was seen to be a produced order, integral and internal (endogenous) to the local settings in which the interaction occurred. That is, it was ongoingly produced in and through the actions of the parties. It was not imposed on them, nor was it a matter of their following some sort of scripts or rules. They were freely involved in that production and were themselves oriented to that production. What they were doing was carrying out actions that were meaningful and consequential for them in that immediate context. They were, for example, opening up conversations, or closing them, or exchanging greetings, or responding to invitations, and so on. (1995:17)

Thus, the study of turn taking initiated the examination of the organisation of social action. Furthermore, this organisation was seen to exhibit sequential characteristics and contextual considerations in and through members' conversational work in accomplishing senses of social order.

The organisation of turn taking (Sacks 1974) is characterised by two components and a corresponding set of rules. These components are known as the turn constructional component (TCC) and the turn allocation component (TAC). The turn constructional component could vary from a single phrase to a full sentence or account. The completion of a TAC, i.e. completing a turn, was followed by a turn transition relevance place (TRP) in which a change of speaker could occur. The turn allocation component is characterised by a number of techniques that can be described by a number of rules for example, i.) current speaker selecting the next speaker and, ii.) current speaker self selecting a next turn.

Turn Taking in the Team Meetings

The prevalence of turn taking can be observed in nearly all aspects of conversation interaction and this includes team meeting talk. As has been stated, within CA, it can be heard to occupy the fundamental sequential method for organising conversation. The use of turn-taking can be observed in the following transcribed data, within which the Team Leader initiates an appeal to members of the team to commit themselves to operating a drop in centre during weekday evenings. The drop in centre has already been organised and is designed as a service through which members of the flood-hit community can access the expertise and help of the flood support team in person.

Example One – Turn Taking in the Team Meeting

1.TL: Any volunteers for the seven thirty till ten shift on Thursday (.)
2.St: Well (.) I'll do it.

Clearly, this example involves a straightforward question/answer adjacency pair. Furthermore, it is observable how they form an adjacency pair a) in terms of the sequential proximity of the next utterance, i.e. they stand beside each other but also in terms of b.) the action predicate 'I'll do it' (L.2), can be heard to be tied to the category 'volunteer' (L.1) and the predicate of the 'seven thirty until ten shift'. In this sense, the predicate of 'I'll do it' is recipiently designed in terms of the predicate of shift work tied to the device 'team'. Consequently, we hear the next part of the adjacency pair as displaying membership of the category 'volunteer' and 'team member'. Thus, the sequential organisation *and* the categorial display are mutually constitutive and are being used in the course of accomplishing the order of allocating activities via this instance of turn-taking.

In the following extract, the discussion concerning the drop in centre (established by the term in order to support flood victims through the provision of advice and other services) and the availability of team members during weekday evenings is heard to exhibit further turn taking amongst team members. This is part of the work of allocating people to times that the drop in centre is to be open to members of the flood-hit community.

Example Two – Turn Taking in the Team Meeting

1.C: I'm quite willing to do that until Seven thirty
2.LVC: I'm still working Friday (.)
3.C: Yes I'll do it until seven thirty =
4.TL: = Friday (2.0) seven thirty[until   ]
5.LVC: [whenever] you want me to do it I'll do it.

In this extract we can hear another form of turn taking in operation. The counsellor states a willingness to work until seven thirty on a project that the team have been discussing, in this instance a drop in centre which will be open for twenty four hours a day. The counsellor's utterance can be heard as a report and as a question about the availability of persons for the twenty four-hour 'drop in' centre. The LVC answers the question, saying he is working on Friday and is therefore available, the counsellor then reaffirms the initial position. The turn taking system here consists of (a.) a statement (b.) a response to the statement and (c.) a reaffirmation of the initial statement. Again, the dual nature of recipiency can be heard to be operating. The adjacency of making a question/statement with an adjoining answer/response and the following reaffirmation of the first statement can be heard as a particular type of turn-taking structure. In categorial terms, the counsellor displays the predicate of 'willingness' alongside the time category of 'until seven thirty' (L.4) (a category of the device time), the LVC's response reflects the initial statement by the counsellor through reference to 'still working' on 'Friday'. In categorial, terms we can hear the relationship between the counsellors utterance and the LVC's utterance as talk between legitimate team members. The counsellors' reaffirmation of her initial utterance then provides the sequential method for hearing the previous two statements as 'going together'. Thus, the two utterances are not only adjacent in terms of the recipient design of the sequential structure, but also in terms of the categories and predicates displayed. The sense of the utterances 'going together' is reinforced through the third part of the sequence, which, whilst repeating the same category work, sequentially displays that the two previous utterances are to be considered together and as referring to exactly the same topic.

This analysis is displayed by the TL's utterance that selects the category 'Friday' from the LVC's utterance and 'seven thirty until' from the counsellor's utterances. The TL's recipiently designed utterance is also posed as a question. It can be heard, in terms of the previous category work, as an invitation to the LVC to speak. That is to say, it forms part of a clearly identifiable and recognisable transitional relevance place for the LVC to take a turn. The TL is not only displaying recognition of the previous sequence, but is also asking the LVC to elaborate on the time that he is available for duty. The LVC, who has already made himself available as a volunteer for the drop in centre, replies in a way which ties the speaker's incumbency with being available for the project after seven thirty on the Friday. Thus, we are met with a statement, response and reaffirmation sequence, which is then followed by a question/answer sequence. Again, within these meeting extracts both categorial and sequential methods are being used in order to make a decision and allocate jobs to be done.

Within the following extract SW1 suggests that the team 'cascades'. This refers to the process of sharing the details, issues and professional problems associated with particular cases that the team members may be 'carrying'. The purpose of this exercise is to share professional experience as a means of improving practice amongst the team members.

Example Three – Turn Taking

1.SW1: When are we going to do the cascade things (1.0) oughtn't be at this
2.   meeting =
3.TL: =Yes (.)
4.SW1: I mean we've prepared them all (0.5) long time hence(.)
5.TL : Yes (.)
6.SW1: Right.

During the course of this extract we can follow the talk in terms of a pattern of adjacency. These patterns of adjacency can be understood as 'turn constructional units' that build up the sequence, however each unit exhibits different forms of adjacency. The SW1 proffers a rhetorical statement in the form of a question that is then followed by a simple affirmative answer to the question by the TL. The SW1 continues by self-selecting a turn, which seeks to describe and 'add weight' to her initial question. The TL responds to the description with a simple affirmation or acknowledgement, a turn that in terms of adjacency is heard to agree with SW1's description of the topic that she had initiated through the initial question. The SW1 then closes this sequence with the utterance 'Right' (L.6). In one sense, we hear this as the closing of the topic (the topic in this case being the initiation of the process known as cascading) and this particular sequence of talk. The closing is followed by a three second pause, this indicates that the topic has been dealt with and that it is time to move on.

Topical Organisation

A further aspect of conversational structure that is relevant to the notion of managing category flow[2] within meeting talk-in-interaction is the concept of topic. Topics are concerned with what it is members are talking about. Topics may include newsworthy items that inform the recognisable features of the interactional moment. For example, opening topics may include reasons for coming around to visit or experiences gathered from 'the weekend' within the circumstances of a friend making a social visit. Topics can be seen as representative of a sequential feature of conversation in that conversation often involves talk around a number of topics. As a consequence of this observation we may note that different topics are opened and closed and form an integral part of the sequential and ultimately temporal organisation of team members' conversation.

Sacks (1991) describes the movement in conversation from one topic to the next as 'topic change'. For Sacks, 'talking topically' does not consist of 'blocks of talk about topic', rather the management of topics is part and parcel of the interactional achievement of conversation. Members cannot assume that the following interlocutor will accept an introduced topic, members' talk, according to Sacks, recognises these problems and members use methods through which topics can be managed. One of the principal ways by which topic change occurs is through the 'touching off' of one topic on to another.[3] According to Coulthard, (1977) topic management may transform into topic conflict within which more than one interlocutor competes for the opening of a particular topic. Conversation may overlap as different interlocutors compete for the floor and even when a speaker manages to introduce or open a topic, co-conversationalists may 'skip connect'. This method involves referring to the 'last but one' utterance, thus an interlocutor may simply ignore the previous utterance which attempts to open a topic by 'reasserting their own' (Coulthard 1977). However, the proximity of the topic openings suggests that they appear to be relatively contextually bound to the conversation at hand.

Another feature of topic identified by Sacks is the notion of topical coherence. For Sacks, this is tied to the methods of categorisation and the rules of application. Topical coherence is a categorical phenomena in terms of category display but it can also be conceptualised as an organising principle in terms of the praxiological considerations described in Sacks' rules of application. Furthermore, the notion of 'category coherence' as an organising principle of topic is, within the work of Harvey Sacks, connected with the more explicit concerns of the social and sequential organisation of conversation.

In this extract, the SW1 is recounting her experience of relationships between team members in different teams that she has worked within. Furthermore, she presents an account of a 'problem' that the first part of the account is used to introduce. The display of such reflexive evaluations by different *individual* team members was not unusual although, as this extract indicates, such topics were seldom 'taken up' by other team members within the meetings.

Example Four – Topic Changing

1.SW1: I personally have found (2.0) I think the relationships were warmer (1.5) I
2.   dunno if anyone else agrees
3.LVC: mmmm (.)
4.SW1:   Very hard to talk seriously in this team (1.0) isn't it =
5.LVC: =Yep
6.SW1:   It's where the issue is (1.0) I think(.)
7.SW3:   I think it did do a good thing in a way [from the wor'   ]
8.TL: [with Karens thi ::]ng (.)
9.SW1:   She's not joining our (0.5) moving into our room.

During the course of this extract, we can observe how the SW1 is concerned with relating an account about her experiences of communication with other social service agencies at other meetings. She states that the 'relationships were warmer' at these encounters (L.1). However, she is not met with a response after providing the question, towards the end of the account, as to 'whether anyone else agrees'. Her invitation to the other participants to speak is not taken up by any other members of the team. Consequently, she shifts topic, that is to say, she re-selects herself to speak again on a next topic, namely the difficulty of 'talking seriously in the team' (L.4) and this being representative of 'where the issue is'. This next topic's 'topical organisation' (category display – in – topic) contrasts with the previous topic's categorial organisation, i.e. 'warmth of relationships' as opposed to difficulty talking 'seriously' within 'this team'.

At this stage the LVC takes a turn (L.5) that leads to a description of the topic of not being able to talk seriously as an 'issue'. Having done this the SW1 self-selects a turn that seeks to address the topic proffered by the last utterance as an 'issue'. However, the interruption (note the overlap) by the TL is representative of a topic change through interruption and 'skip connecting' from the first utterance by the SW1 in which she referred to her experience of interactions with other agencies working within the community. The TL refers to 'Karen's thing', we hear this as a description of the SW1's account of her experiences. However, by referring back to the initial utterance (and hence topic) the TL switches the topic from the 'issue', i.e. talking seriously in the team, back to the initial, relatively safe topic of the SW1's initial account. The SW1 responds to the TL's interruption, question-based topic change by stating that 'Karen' (possibly a potential inter-agency worker or potential secondment) is not coming to work from the same premises.

The following extract exhibits further aspects of topic conflict within talk. During this extract, the team are discussing the topic of smoking and the location of smokers and non-smokers within different parts of the building. Certain members of the team who do not smoke are attempting to secure a specific part of the building as a non-smoking area. The topic of smoking is interesting here, as it could be heard to involve a specific type of organisational talk and the social geography of the team within the building. Indeed, the topic of smoking is not discussed in a jocular fashion. Within the work place it is viewed as an important work issue within the teams day to day work activities.

Example Five – Topic Conflict

1.SW3: I'm (0.5) I'd want assurances that the room upstairs would be no smoking
2. and no smoking in absence either =
3.TL: = mm =
4.SW3: = cos you come back often and there's smoking been going on
5. and you walk into it anyway (.)
6.C: That's been the nice thing about our room
7.SW3: Yes (.)
8.C: [It's that there's been] no smoking
9.SW3: [Yes especially in   ]
10.CDW:If you do [tha'   ]
11.C: [People] have to smoke I can appreciate that
12. y'know but I don't want to sit there.

In this extract the topic is smoking, in particular the activity of smoking in a shared facility. An account is assembled through a collection of 'utterances' (a process which I will discuss in more detail at a later stage during this book). However, having assembled the account around the topic, the CDW attempts to make a bid for the floor through interrupting the SW3 who has been jointly producing an account on a turn by turn basis with the counsellor. At this point, the counsellor interrupts the CDW by stating that she appreciates that 'people have to smoke' but not in her environment. The person hearably attended to is not specified but we hear it, through adjacency and recipient design, as including the CDW. Indeed, by attempting to select himself to speak (and 'change' topic) he fills the conversational availability of the incumbency of a person who smokes in the room in question, i.e. by recognising the TRP as his point to speak. The topic conflict occurs between his interruption of the SW3 and the subsequent interruption by the counsellor. In one sense, by recognising the TRP as his point to speak, the counsellor uses it as a resource (sufficient evidence of inclusion of the membership category and the predicate of smoking in the room in question) to close the exchange.

Within this next extract a member of the team initiates a topic. The topic involves initiating a form of team activity that involves exchanging accounts about interesting cases in order to exchange expertise and views on particularly challenging or difficult aspects of their casework. Such activities were not commonly observed within the Flood Support Team although members did acknowledge that an exchange of views about aspects of casework often occurred in non-formal settings such as the coffee room or corridor. However, such non-formal situated work was outside the parameters of this study although its professed existence was brought to my attention. Within this example (that includes and leads on from the data fragment presented in example three), the topic of carrying out a formal exchange of views (namely 'cascading') and the subsequent response to the suggestion could be explained in terms of the above. However, my concern here is not with the *why* but with the *how*.

Example Six – Closing Down a Topic

1.SW1: When are we going to do the cascade things (1.0) oughtn't be at
2.   this meeting =
3.TL: =Yes (.)
4.SW1: I mean we've prepared them all (0.5) long time hence(.)
5.TL : Yes (.)
6.SW1: Right
7.   (3.0)
8.SW1: More bloody skills you mean (laughter)
9.TL: It's time to cascade (.)
10.SW2:er hmmm (.)
11.SW3:[mm   ]
12.St: [mm   ]
13.C: [mmm =]
14.TL: = Can we cascade in our thoughts
15.   (sound of shuffling and chairs moving)
16.SW1:Can we (1.0) also need some sharing of cases that are particularly

17.   difficult (0.4) interesting (1.0) cos I don't think we do enough of
18.   that (0.5) except informally often there are learning points (.)
19.TL: What are you desperate to learn
20.   (laughter)
21.St: Yes (.) but it should be casual
22.   (7.0).

During the course of the conversation two topics are initiated. Firstly, the opening statement (L.1) introduces the topic of holding a cascading session during the meeting. Once this is established between the Team Leader and SW1 (L.1-L.4), it provides an utterance which can be heard as a prompt for people to take a turn and therefore cascade by providing accounts of cases that they are involved in (L.9). The responses provided by the team members present can be heard as taking a turn (i.e. recognising the TRP) but not orienting themselves toward the recipiently designed features of the TL's request. That is to say, not taking up the invitation to speak in a way which recognisably conforms to the activity of cascading. This is made recognisable by the TL's following utterance 'Can we cascade in our thoughts then' (L.14). Clearly, this makes recognisable that the predicate of cascading consists of providing accounts concerning cases and not thinking about them. The SW1 attempts to reinitiate the form of talk described as cascading by providing an account of cascading (L.16 to 18). We hear that cascading may involve the sharing of difficult or interesting cases that can facilitate the desired predicate of learning. The SW1 states that this process occurs informally but not in formal contexts. The use of the contrast class can be heard as a means of documenting, and re-emphasising what type of talk is required to accomplish cascading. This account is met by a question by the TL that changes the topic (L.19). By questioning an aspect of the category coherence of the SW1 account (namely the reference to 'learning' which is tied to the category of states of mind i.e. being desperate) the initiated topic of cascading is re-orientated. This reorientation is met by laughter, the student (L.21) continues by referring to the term 'casual', which we may hear as meaning that the process should be informal. The use of this predicate may be seen as a strategy for 'going off topic'. The student's utterance asserts that the form of talk being pointed to and requested at this point 'should be casual'. This is then followed by a seven second pause and a topic change that concerns phone messages and team member availability. Thus, the team members go off topic and use the category of 'casual' as a means of closing down the proposed topical talk which the SW1 ties to the process of 'cascading'.

Stories, Accounts and Extended Sequences

A further feature of talk-in-interaction within meetings can be found in the elicitation and display of extended sequences. These sequences include accounts and stories, these serve to perform a variety of tasks and accomplish a number of ends. The examination of stories and accounts within team meeting settings will be explored in detail during the course of chapter six. However, some general observations about story type utterances will be made at this stage. In the following extract the lay volunteer co-ordinator relates a story about a client and the movement of furniture during the initial flooding. This story exhibits a number of story type characteristics. It also relays important information about a client who is known to the team.

Example Seven – Extended Sequences, Stories and Accounts

1.LVC: Oh that's Mrs ***** for you though (.) the one we are dealing
2.   with (.) lives on Queens road (.) we love the old lady (.) that's her
3.   sister who lives on Craig y Don (.) now
4.   then when she was flooded we had to take it to her sisters first (.)
5.   unload it there (.) unload it there then let her sister check it first
6.   then get her sister around Craig y Don (.) and the
7. SW1: [You have qualifications for this then]
8.LVC: [Her older sister said yes the other one] was allowed to have the
9.   furniture (2.0) so
10.   then we took it around to Mrs *****
11.SW1:How do you spell (name of clients) =

During the course of this extract the extended sequence elicited by the LVC displays a story preface (L.1). This preface consists of locating the client in terms of the stage of life device (old lady), her place of residence, the volunteers attitude towards her and some information about her family connections (L.2). This is followed by the story proper signalled by the utterance 'now then' (L.3), the story proper consists of information about the movement and storage of furniture during the flooding and a conversation/negotiation with the client and the clients sister regarding the storage of the salvaged furniture (L.4, 7). The story closes with a reference to the furniture and its eventual storage at the client's sister's house (L.7). The display of stories and accounts of team meetings is a general characteristic of such settings. They remain important conversational methods for exchanging information and communicating important 'background' information about clients. Furthermore, the multilayered character of team members' talk also leads to an appreciation of such methods in relation to interactional issues surrounding team roles, knowledge and claims making.

Preliminary Observational Investigations: Some Considerations

During this preliminary application of sequential and categorial analysis of team meeting talk a number of points may be put forward. The examination of meetings has often ignored the local conversational machinery of meetings as situated accomplishments of an ongoingly achieved and interactionally constituted order. The spectre of external considerations has been expressed in terms of specified grammars for interaction within meetings. The description of the meeting as a resource for multidisciplinary teamwork has taken notions such as dialogue, understanding, meaning and the exchange of information for granted. The examination of the local conversational machinery of meetings provides for a respecification of such theorised descriptions by illustrating the way in which members utilise specific methods in attempting to deal with the emergent contingencies of doing the order of a meeting. Indeed, by locating such emergent properties within the context of members praxiological work the possibility of investigating processes which are fundamental to teamwork can be realised. Much of the literature dealing with teamwork does not examine those processes but assume they are present. The precise details of how such generalised descriptions tally with the lived work of doing team meetings remains unspecified, poorly documented and misunderstood.

During the course of this chapter I have sought to illustrate, through references to transcribed examples collected from the field, some of the methods through which multidisciplinary meetings are socially and interactionally achieved. Furthermore, I have sought to focus on the local, in situ use, by members, of specific conversational methods and strategies in carrying out a range of activities. I have also sought to indicate the way in which categories-in-talk, as category flow (Watson 1997) or display are realised and are managed in and through sequential methods of conversational organisation. This chapter has also begun the process of respecifying multidisciplinary social work practice within the context of the meeting as an activity that is grounded within an array of conversational work and praxiological considerations by members, rather than externalised social forces or exogenously described pre-programmed professional behaviour resulting from a *causal* relationship arising from the previous training or experience of team members. By focussing on the local management of categories I hope to have emphasised the need to focus on multidisciplinary practice, within the context of meetings, as opposed to people's 'internal states of mind', as an endogenously, in situ and locally produced phenomena. Furthermore, by examining the situated character of team members talk I have sought to illustrate the way in which the formalised, 'institutional' character of such talk relies on the situated specifics of team members praxiological methods. Thus, the notion that the methods used are distinct from ordinary conversation, as the Institutional Talk Program maintains, is questioned. Clearly, the contextual arrangements provide a resource which can be appealed to and made relevant through situated work. However, the sequential and categorial features of such talk are situated rather than institutional. Institutionality is a device that may be oriented to by members within team meeting talk, however, this does not suggest that Institutionality is a consistently and monolithically installed feature of members talk. Thus, from the position of a reconsidered model of membership categorisation analysis Hester and Francis (forthcoming) state:

> It follows from the unique adequacy feature that each enquiry must in significant respects be distinct; there can be no generic 'method' across different phenomena. The analytic approach taken in one enquiry is not 'exportable' from its original field of application, *however successful it may have been there*, to studies in a different field ... In the course of its (ITP's) attempts to apply the methods and concepts of conversation analysis to the study of 'institutional' activities, where this term is a gloss for medical, journalistic, educational, judicial, and so forth, the very character of the phenomenon disappears from view.

This point is echoed by Lynch and Bogen (1997) who argue that the invocation of a contextual backdrop to talk (institutional or otherwise) is an attempt to introduce second order or generic explanations to bare on members situated activities, even if one accepts the possibility of wider contextual parameters influencing members actions (rather than social order being locally accomplished by members) Lynch and Bogen (1997:276) state:

> The generic domain of conversation is not the only relevant backdrop against which singular events take on their specificity and sensibility.

Having applied some of the principles and methods discussed in chapter two in order to illustrate some basic characteristics of the social organisation of meeting talk I will now seek to examine the ethnomethodological dimensions and interactional accomplishment of roles in teams. In short I will seek to respecify some of the basic criteria which were evident during the previous discussion of multidisciplinarity and team.

The notion of team roles was a central features of the models and ideas explored. I use the notion of respecification in a way that corresponds to the notion of deconstructing foundational concepts through the analysis of practical action (Jayussi 1991). In doing so, I will seek to examine the haecceitic achievement of interactional orders, which in the generalising mode of sociological enquiry constitute social roles, professional/non-professional knowledge and ways of validating such knowledge in terms of theoretical structures and external, exogenous causal explanations. In examining the fine detail of interactional work as an ongoing process of haeccetic assemblages of order it is hoped that the routinised and taken for grantedness of role work in teams will be illustrated. It is to this area of social organisation in multidisciplinary team meeting settings that we now turn.

Notes

1   A comprehensive discussion of recipient design can be found in Sacks's Lectures in Conversation (1992). The notion of recipience is being invoked here in order to prepare ground for a more thorough discussion of the local production of conversation and the socially dynamic organising principle of recognisability.

2   This term is used to describe the occurrence of categories, predicates and devices within conversation. Furthermore it seeks to illustrate the way in which clusters of categories have to be managed in terms of praxiological considerations (Sacks rules of application and recipient design) and the associated considerations of sequential organisation e.g. conforming to the expectations of a first part of an adjacency pair. In this sense the raw material of 'know-how' and 'knowledge' (i.e. a set of categories which predicate a specific set of relationships that convey an internal logic and make ontological and epistemological claims about phenomena) can be seen to be managed by praxiological and sequential methods of conversational organisation.

3   This method involves the production of category relevance within the earlier part of the topics' delivery. If the topic is managed and/or organised in a story format we might conceive to situate category relevant material within the preface. However having made such category relevance recognisable the dual function of relevance has to be realised through a topic shift (and consequently a category shift) that remains associated and intelligible to the listener and listeners in terms of the in situ conversational fabric.

4 Role as an Interactional Device in Multidisciplinary Team Practice

In this chapter I intend to examine the lived character of role within multidisciplinary team practice. I intend to contrast the lived orderliness of role work with models of role and practice evident within some of the models of multidisciplinary practice outlined during the introduction to this book. A starting point in this endeavour will be a consideration of the concept of role in the social sciences. A consideration of the concept of role in the social sciences is central to contrasting the models of role evident in models of multidisciplinary practice with the character of first order observations of interaction in teams. This is because the concept and articulation of team roles evident within the multidisciplinary team literature is based on the traditional social scientific concepts of role that I intend to explore prior to analysis of examples of the social organisation and accomplishment of role in team based settings. I will then contrast these models with the notion of role as an interactional device and outline what this concept means through the analysis of talk in interaction within multidisciplinary social/care work team meetings, although some indirect discussion and explanation of this concept will be presented as a preface to analysis.

Role Theory and the Human Sciences

The concept of role is one that has become axiomatic to the social science tradition. It serves as a useful method through which human behaviour and action can be tied to the wider conceptualisation of social structure. Furthermore, it is also deployed as a device for describing individual action not only in the context of the social, but also in terms of institutions and organisations. However, the concept of 'role', whilst relatively stable, can be viewed as being developed and promoted within the human sciences through a number of identifiable traditions. These include, the anthropological legacy, structural functionalism, social psychology, symbolic interactionism and social constructionism, each of these will be briefly considered before the ethnomethodological approach to role, adopted in this book, is specified.

The Anthropological Legacy

The anthropological work of Malinowoski (1944) provides one of the most well known examinations of roles and his studies of social relations within 'simple' and 'complex' societies. From a general anthropological point of view, role provides a useful 'intellectual tool' (Banton 1965) for analysing social organisation. Furthermore, within the anthropological tradition role is realised in terms of complimentary relationships (e.g. leader and follower). Such relationships (the 'dyads' of social psychology) are seen to underpin the altruistic and egoistic dimensions of co-operation. Ralph Linton (1936) used the concept of 'role' in an anthropological textbook *'The Study of Man'*. Linton's view of role was tied to the concept of status, consequently Linton was concerned with examining role in terms of wider society. As Banton (1965:29) notes, it was Linton who introduced the demarcation of role into an *ascribed* and *achieved* form of classification. Furthermore, Linton (1933) and Banton (1963) recognise that social role may be varied and diverse, an incumbent may carry out a range of different roles. Banton (1963) describes this as the 'role set' (1963:26) which social actors may inhabit. According to Banton (1963:30) roles must also be understood in terms of kinship, ethnic, economic, political, ritual, religious and recreational considerations. This approach was to influence later work, which can be broadly described as the Structural Functionalist approach.

Structural Functionalism

The notion of social role is a familiar spectre to students of Parsonian functionalism. For Parsons (1951), roles were normative entities that, in the case of gender for example, were the product of socialisation. Roles could also be allocated via meritocratic sub-systems such as 'education'. Such an allocation of roles was contextualised under the rubric of some reinforcing socialising process or 'secondary socialisation'. Within the structural functionalist model the social system was seen to consist of a network of relationships at the level of society's integral components. From a structural functionalist perspective these 'processes of interaction between actors' were the essential structure of the social system. From Parsons' point of view (1951:25) the motif of participation by actors within the plurality of 'interactive relationships' was of supreme significance, participation was mediated through two considerations:

> ... participation in turn has two principal aspects. On the one hand there is the positional aspect – that of where the actor in question is 'located' in the social system relative to other actors. This is what we call his 'status', which is his place in the relationship system considered as a structure, that is a patterned system of parts. On the other hand there is the processual aspect, that of what the actor does in his relations with others seen in the context of it's functional significance for the social system. It is this which we call role.

Within this theoretical schema the notion of 'role' and 'status' are distinct from the notion of 'personality', furthermore the concept of 'status' is associated with 'role'. However status is seen is viewed as an objective manifestation of social structure whilst role is compromised by the subjective criteria involved in 'playing out a role'. However, Parsons maintains that the status-role axis is firmly contextualised within the social system and is analogous to the conceptualisation of the 'particle' in physics. Furthermore, role is also regulated via the wider structural pre-requisite of pattern maintenance and the social-psychological processes of positive and negative sanctioning. For Parsons the social-psychological dimensions of role provide for his fundamental account of the interactional order. Consequently Parsons (1951:26) refines his notion of role in terms of:

> ... a sector of the total orientation system of an individual actor which is organised about expectations in relation to a particular interaction context, that is integrated with a particular set of value standards which govern interaction with one or more alters in the appropriate complimentary role.

Thus, roles are entities which are manifest within the different institutions that constitute the social system (e.g. the family or the education system) which actors convey and display during the course of goal orientated activities. 'Roles' and 'status' are thus conceived as a cluster of norms mediated and realised through process i.e. social action. From a structural functionalist point of view the 'role-status' matrix is a demonstrable feature of the very foundations of social order. Furthermore, whilst Parsons conceptualisation of role involves a degree of plurality (e.g. the division between public and private roles which can be simultaneously occupied by a given social actor) it remains rigid in terms of its discursive ependence on systemic conceptualisations of the social.

Parsons' notion of role and status as distinct from personality does not mean that such a relationship between these social variables is unimportant. Whilst the precise quantification of personality remains problematic it is certainly seen to have an effect on 'role-expectation'. Other aspects of role that Parsons examines include 'role-differentiation', 'role-conflict' and 'role ambiguity'. In one sense, it is the relationship between role, status and society that crystallises functionalism's 'action frame of reference'. It is Parsons' conceptualisation of role-status that enables the integration of the biological and psychological properties of the human organism into the social structure. To put it another way, it is this relationship which, via normative considerations, is axiomatic to the human organism and the social. It is this conceptualisation of role, status and personality that enables Parsons to bridge the gap between biological drives and the normative social order. This is achieved through the consideration of the above and the invocation of an all embracing inclusive category of subjectivity, namely the social actor! A discursive entity that mediates biological/psychological drives via the interactive process of role and orientation to the 'other' and the mutual recognition of the inter-subjective normative entity of 'status' with all its 'objective' and palpable social significance. Parsons bridges the gap, in the last analysis, by utilising social psychological principles that I will now, briefly, discuss and describe.

Social Psychology

Despite the fact that this thesis is not concerned with psychology in any way, shape or form we cannot ignore its contribution to 'role theory'. Much of the social-psychological work on role can easily 'slot into' the Parsonian plenum. It attempts to document the relationship between psychological characteristics (i.e. personality) with the wider social structure and the more immediate environment of institutions and the private sphere of family life.

An individual role is, in one sense, the manner through which the psychological make up of individuals negotiate social contexts via specific social scripts. Furthermore, social psychological versions of role theory (Biddle 1979) also advance the claim that an individual's psychological characteristics can be predicated via attention to their social position and/or context (the inference being that the converse relationship, as representative of the Parsonian notion of 'role-expectation' has empirical/scientist validity). The pattern of people's behaviour is seen to have a meaningful correlation with the patterns of social context. Individuals' behaviour is seen to be a product of their socialisation and the positive and negative sanctioning procedures of social organisation.

Symbolic Interactionism

The concept of role within symbolic interactionism is central to the theoretical and ethnographic work of Becker, Mead, Blumer, Strauss and the later work of Goffman. In Goffman's (1968) study of total institutions, the concept of role was explored in terms of ritual, and the interactional presentation of 'self' within such settings. For Goffman and the interactionist tradition, the concept of role is one that is not fixed, but is conceptualised as an interactional framework that is constantly being negotiated between social actors within interaction. The dramaturgical analogy provides for a way of conceptualising the interactional order as one within which social actors put on a performance. Goffman also draws attention to the instrumental, strategic and pragmatic dimensions of social life. With respect to his analysis of total institutions Goffman draws our attention to the way in which roles can be understood in terms of impression management. For example, the competency of medical staff and the relationship between staff and patients is something that is interactionally achieved and is not imposed by some structural apparatus. Within this metaphor Goffman invokes the additional concepts of ritual and game theory. As Sharrock et al (1992) note, Goffman's use of game theory provides for a reading of interaction in instrumental terms in which the notion of strategy and moves are used to explain social action. In contrast to this, the notion of ritual provides for a more expressive picture of interaction within which the expression or presentation of 'self' is realised. Thus the interactionist conceptualisation of role can be seen to be tied to a range of sophisticated and detailed analytical metaphors which help to illustrate the accomplished character of roles within institutional and non-institutional settings.

Social Constructionism

In Berger and Luckmannn's (1966) book *The Social Construction of Reality* we are presented with a theoretical approach which advances the claim that reality is socially constructed. Furthermore, it is, they argue, the task of the sociology of knowledge to analyse the process through which reality constructed. For Berger and Luckmann, roles are important within what they describe as the 'institutional order'. Within this frame of reference 'forms of action are typified'. For Berger and Luckmann, social action requires typification in order to reify specific forms of action, to endow them with an 'objective sense'. According to Berger and Luckmann

(1966:90), this involves 'linguistic objectification'. They argue that such a process constitutes:

> an identification of the self with the objective sense of the action; the action that is going on determines, for that moment, the self-apprehension of the actor, and does so in the objective sense that has been socially ascribed to the action.

Thus, the process of the social actor identifying with 'objectivated typifications of conduct' is seen as a reflexive process of displaying different 'types'. This dynamic is viewed as the underlying process of carrying out a role. Roles are the result of a phenomenological and linguistic process that, as Berger and Luckmann (1966:91) put it:

> ... occurs in the context of an objectified stock of knowledge common to a collectivity of actors. Roles are types of actors in such a context.

Furthermore, with reference to wider social considerations, Berger and Luckmann (1996:91), echoing Parsons (albeit within a phenomenological and linguistic matrix of reconsideration), continue by stating:

> It can readily be seen that the construction of role typologies is a necessary correlate of the institutionalisation of conduct. Institutions are embodied in individual experience by means of roles. The roles, objectified linguistically, are an essential ingredient of the objectively available world of any society. By playing roles, the individual participates in a social world. By internalising these roles, the same world becomes subjectively real to him.

Berger and Luckmann (1966:92) see roles as the 'nexus' by which the totality of the social whole is realised. Indeed in terms of the sociology of knowledge the analysis of roles is:

> ... of particular importance to the sociology of knowledge because it reveals the mediations between the macroscopic universes of meaning objectivated in a society and the ways by which these universes are subjectively real to individuals.

That is to say, roles represent the epistemological dynamic through which social constructionism can represent itself as a theoretical device for accounting for the subjective, phenomenological experience of social interaction with the objectivist sense of social structure. In short, it encapsulates Berger and Luckmann's re-reading of the Schutzian phenomenological notion of role as a bridging device between the epistemological, ontological disputes in the macro-micro debate of their sociological moment.

Role as an Interactional Device

The notion of 'role' as an interactional device was developed within Halkowski's (1990: 565) ground breaking paper in which he proposes the following analytical consideration:

> Rather than treating "role" as a self evident, social-scientific resource for analysis, and following the work by Garfinkel (1967) and Zimmerman and Pollner (1970), social scientists should take it as a topic of study. Doing so will help illuminate how interactants organise the social world by their use of these conceptions and actions.

This orientation towards examining 'role' as a member's phenomena can be operationalised through the utilisation of Conversation Analysis and Membership Categorisation Analysis. Indeed, at a later stage in this chapter I will aim to explore the discursive and interactional characteristics of role as a situated members device.

Halkowski's work is a good example of this approach. He examined recordings of the Iran Contra Hearings held in Washington DC and, through the analysis of transcripts, illustrated how role-identity categories are used as a resource by interlocuters for 'category shifting', as a means of dodging allegations and shifting blame. For Halkowski (1990), Hilbert (1981:216) accurately sums up the use of 'role' as a resource for members:

> Our recommendation is to view "role" as an organising concept used on occasion by actors in social settings, and to view its utility for actors in terms of what they can do with it; i.e. the work they require it to do, in sustaining the perceived stability of social behaviour, whatever their immediate purposes. Viewed this way, roles are not behavioural matrices to be described and explained but are conceptual resources actors use to clear up confusion, sanction troublemakers, instruct others in the ways of the world, and so forth.

As an interactional device and resource, we can begin to consider role as a means through which members practically, and locally accomplish, a sense of social order. Halkowski's description of 'role' as an interactional device can therefore be understood as a logical extension of Garfinkel's concern with the way in which members use methods to impose order in the world. Thus 'role', as deployed by members, can be viewed as a method for accounting for underlying patterns, pointing to regularities and interactionally establishing, negotiating and achieving a locally produced sense of social order.[1] Consequently, it is in this way that I will seek to examine the accomplishment and utilisation of role within a series of multidisciplinary team meetings and interactions gathered from the case explored in the course of this book.

Analysis

The following extract is taken from a team meeting and involves a discussion that concerns the deployment of different team members within the community in the light of a decision to initiate a drop in centre for the following week.

Example One – Team Meeting

1.LVC : Aren't we going to be overstreched because (1.5) say I end up in
2.   Glanarfon (1.5) if someone comes in there (whose) got a serious
3.   problem (coughing)
4.SW1: Not talking about your (.) your own problem?
5.   (laughter)
6.LVC: Sorry I wouldn't know how to deal with it (2.0) I'm not trained in it =
7.SW1: = But (name of Team Leader) is saying there is going to be two people (.)
8.LVC: Ahhh (3.0) I'm sorry.

This extract contains an utterance that can be heard to contrast between the 'role-identity' of lay and professional workers. The LVC discusses a perceived 'problem', an activity associated with the practices and aims of doing a team meeting. The LVC informs members at the Team meeting that if he was 'out in the field' and encountered a 'serious problem' he would feel unable to adequately deal with the problem presented. Furthermore, the LVC is heard to make certain reports concerning the extent of his remit (L.1-2). The first interjection by SW1 is heard as a joke or humorous comment and is followed by laughter from other members of the team (L.4-5). It provides for the predicate of training to be reselected by the previous speaker in his following utterance (L.6). Furthermore, it is the topic of category warrantability (the category in question being one's role-identity within the Team) that is made recognisable by SW1's utterance. It makes recognisable that the predicate of 'not being trained' is being tied to the LVC (in that they are volunteers and are not professional workers). The warrantability of the LVC category incumbency and the achieved predicate of 'not being trained' are then co-selected with an inability to deal (L.6) with 'serious problems' in the field.

The problem talk elicits further solutions to the issue presented. This is made available through an informing procedure, which also involves the use of categories of population and pro-terms, that provide and display the distinctions in category warrantability between team members in the subsequent talk transcribed and presented in the following data extract. Here, the conversational exchange involves a concern about volunteers working within the community and encountering situations or requests from flood victims that require professional assistance, advice or support. The volunteer co-ordinators working alongside the LVC are not, it is reported, able to respond to such requests or situations. This is due to their category incumbency (i.e. not occupying a professional position) and inability to make responses that can be sanctioned in terms of statutory procedures or be represented as professional advice. It is this problem that the LVC has brought to the attention of the team.

Example Two – Team Meeting

1. SW1: I'll go with you (name of LVC) =
2. LVC: = If you do that (2.0) so there's somebody else there (1.0) you know (1.5)
3.   cos
4. C: [Oh yes we would do th: :a:t   ]
5. LVC: [every volunteer coordinator should   ] have a social worker (1.2) sort of
6.   thing
7.   hh::mm.

This talk, which follows the previous extract, provides for a complex process of identity work and the accomplishment and display of relevant team membership categories. Firstly, the counsellor embellishes the LVC reference to 'if you do that' (L.2) by selecting the pro-term 'we' (L.4) in providing a solution to the proffered problem at hand. The pro-term 'we' is heard to differentiate between the lay worker and the professional. This is made recognisable by the recipient design of the utterances between the LVC, the social worker and counsellor within which 'we' is heard to refer to the counsellor and social worker but not the lay volunteer[s]. This conversational device is recognisably oriented to at the end of this extract via the LVC's closing recommendation (L.5, 6), that every volunteer co-ordinator should have 'a social worker sort of thing.'

Thus, the term 'we' operates as a method for concretising the display of distinct predicates, with regard to training and dealing with serious problems, and the role-category incumbency and warrantability of the lay worker and the professionals within the team. This 'role-identity' categorisation work is initially made recognisable by the LVC, through reference to the perceived requirement of the professional team member to be alongside lay volunteers in the field. Thus, the contrast class of lay worker and professional is achieved through the *tying of specific in situ predicates (e.g. 'being trained' and 'dealing with serious problems')* to the specific job titles. Whilst explicit references to the role-identity categories of 'professional' and 'lay worker' remain unstated, the predicate contrast reflexively points to the availability of such a category as a member's methodical concern. This process of different identifications, and hence different competencies and expectations, provides for the mutually elaborative establishment of 'difference' between team members and the role categories of lay and professional workers. This practical accomplishment provides for an example of the weak form of recognisability: that is to say whilst the category distinction is not explicitly referred to it is made recognisable through reference to the distinction in the activities and properties associated with the different members of the team.

The problem of providing care or help for people 'with serious problems' is one context within which the distinction between the lay and professional members of the team is interactionally realised and locally achieved. During the course of the meeting this distinction is used as a further resource, by the LVC, in elaborating the boundaries and competencies of the category incumbency (and more precisely the category warrantability) within which they speak and act as members of the *Team*. The following extract includes, and leads on from, the previous extract and involves the LVC expressing, to the team, his analysis of the problem of role-category incumbency (in this case the position of lay volunteer) and his experience of interacting with flood victims without the category resource of professional status.

Example Three – Team Meeting

1.LVC: Every volunteer coordinator should have a social worker (.) sort of thing (.)
2.   hhmm =
3.SW1: = Personal to them (.)
4.LVC: Mmmmm
5.   (laughter)
6.SW2: Why not? (1.0)
7.   (laughter)
8.LVC: The only concern I would say (3.0) is if you ended up (1.0) with two
9.   there (1.5) who wouldn't (0.5) y'know (1.5) I wouldn't come (1.0)
10.   if somebody came (1.5) if we did see somebody (1.0) and we were
11.   really concerned(2.0) I would be worried of saying the wrong thing anyway
12.   (1.0) 'pull yourself together' (3.0) hmph (2.0) it's the next thousand years

13.   you have got to wait for (2.0)
14.   [laughter   ]
15.   [don't worry] about this year (.) but if I did say the wrong thing it would
16.   reflect back on the Team anyway.

This account, which follows the previous extracts (example one and two), includes a recognisable display of the methods and strategies discussed in the initial stages of this chapter. Furthermore, in Sacksian terms it exhibits 'second story' characteristics. The reference to the recommendation that every volunteer co-ordinator should have a 'social worker sought of thing' can be heard to be responded to by a recipiently designed category selection that is provided by the SW1 (L.3). This response recognises the topical coherence of the LVC's recommendation. However, the recommendation is repeated as a preface to the LVC's account (L.8-13), alongside the situated incumbent predicate of 'concern'. It is also used to 'touch off' a different topic. This topic involves the invocation of a further set of predicates that are tied to role-identity category warrantability and incumbency of the Lay Volunteer. In this instance the account relates the possibility of being 'in the field' and 'saying the wrong thing' to a member of the community with the aforementioned category interacting with a potential client with 'serious problems'. In a second story format the SW1 seeks to embellish the predicates of the role-identity category of 'lay volunteer'. This involves 'not being trained' to deal with serious problems, not having qualifications (and therefore not ascribing to the available category of 'professional'). The predicates of saying the 'right' or 'wrong' thing, on the other hand, are invoked by the LVC as his method for distinguishing between the professional social workers and the role identity of a volunteer co-ordinator. Furthermore, the final lines of the account (L. 15-16) also refer to saying the 'wrong thing' and such a course of action 'reflecting back on the team'. Thus, the predicate of saying the wrong thing, once tied to the membership category of 'volunteer co-ordinator', is also heard to implicate 'reflecting back on the team' as a whole. In terms of membership categorisation, the predicate of 'reflecting' back on the team is device based (the device being the 'team') of which the incumbent speaker (i.e. the LVC) is a membership category (Watson 1978).

Other categories within this device include the role-identity categories of 'professional', 'lay volunteer', 'counsellor', 'community development worker', 'social worker' and the 'team leader'. Whilst the above categories are not a constantly and monolithically interactionally installed feature of multidisciplinary talk, they are made available in terms of similar category warrantability and incumbency work displayed and discussed above, i.e. the endogenous and local interaction pertaining to competencies, attributes and expectations of different team members.

Role-Category Identity as a Member's Phenomena

Other examples of role-identity category work involve the use of the omni-relevant device of the 'team' in suggesting courses of action and describing problems and troubles of team members. The following extract involves an account of the Counsellor's experience of her category incumbency being invoked by members of the flood hit community whilst not being, in her view, on duty.

Example Four – Allocation Meeting

1.C: A lot of people (1.5) if their there they will unload it (0.4) that's why I don't
2.   walk through the estate at the weekend anymore (1.5) I've had to a-c-t-u-a-l-l-y
3.   stop doing that (1.9) because I know people (1.0) stopping (0.5) not just clients
4.   of mine (0.5) just people (1.0) because they know I work for this team.

As an utterance, we may hear it in terms of what Sacks would call 'problem talk'. The problem being identified is the problem of category incumbency, i.e. being 'a team member' and the implied predicates of this membership category device 'people of the estate', that includes the membership categories of 'clients' and 'non-clients'. Therefore, in one sense, the account provides a rich ethnographic gloss by the *team member* in which the counsellor describes a story which makes recognisable a team members' perception of 'people unloading' requests and problems on them. We are told that this results in the *reported* decision of having to stop walking through the estate. At the end of the account (L.4), an explanation for the account is proffered, this involves a reference to the team members' role-identity category incumbency as a membership category of the device 'team'. This is presented as the reason for the actions reported within the account. Consequently, we may infer that the predicates of being a member of the 'flood support' team is resulting in problems and troubles, for the team member who is reporting the account, during 'the weekend'. This, in turn, can be heard as a membership category of the device 'non-working time'. In other words, people on the estate do not, according to the counsellor's account, suspend the role-identity category of the counsellor as a member of the Flood Support Team and the associated predicates of team members supporting the flood hit community. It must be emphasised that the utterance is an account by a team member rather than a general discussion of professional 'dilemmas'. However, it serves to illustrate the manner through which role-identity category incumbency, associated predicates and the interactional nature of such presentations is, in the case of team members, a member's phenomenon. Indeed, from an ethnographic point of view it is reported, via the counsellor's account, as a phenomenon for people in the community, although this stands outside my concern with transcribed data and locally produced interaction.

Further examples of role-identity category work also surround different team members and contexts. In the case of the allocation meetings, 'professionals' (more specifically those professionals statutorily empowered to make referral and allocation decisions) are in attendance. The discussion surrounds the supervision of a placement order by one of the professionals present. Furthermore, the warrantable activities of the social workers (and the other professionals present) are made topical, and are discussed. The activity of supervising a placement order is made topical by the fact that SW1 has not carried out this activity in the past. Consequently, it provides for some conversation (and category work) within which the role category incumbency of the interlocuters is discussed, and therefore, interactionally established.

Example Five – Allocation Meeting

1.TL: Yeah (1.5) a placement order needs to be supervised (name of SW1)
2.   would like to supervise the placement order (.)
3.SW1: I have never done that =
4.TL: = I know
5.C: (.) It's a learning experience
6.TL: [It's a learning experience   ]
7.C: [It's a learning experience   ]
8.SW1: (name of SW2) what does it involve
9.SW2: Supervising (.) visiting (.) making sure he's alright
10.SW1: Is he still on an order? (.)
11.TL: He is yes (.) he's placed at home
12.SW1: Maybe what I should do is go to the (surname of client) and explain to them
13.   and ask them whether or not they would like me to be the person to do it =
14.SW2: = D'don't they get a choice? =
15.TL: = No (0.4) they do [n't normally get a choice   ]
16.SW1   [But as they know me from] another context they
17.   might feel it would be difficult for me to switch hats from being (0.9)
18.   responsible to the Child Supervisor.

In this extract, questions surrounding role-identity categories are explicitly addressed. The question by the SW1 (L.8) can be heard as an explicit request for a description of the role of supervising a placement order. The second part of the adjacency pair (L.9) by SW2 is a three-part list of descriptive predicates. The utterance at (L.12, 13) regarding a possible visit to the parents by SW1 to explain the particular professional role is heard to be the location, identification and preface to a 'problem'. The problem is then made recognisable at (L.16) through reference to the clients' 'knowing' SW1 from a different context (namely a role as a support worker to the child care supervisor). The problem centres around 'the difficulty' for the SW1 to 'switch hats'. Whilst this does not conform to the role-identity category work between team members as such, it constitutes interactional and conversational work in pursuing a particular type of role-identity category warrantability, namely supervising a placement order. Furthermore, the reference to the problem of adopting a different role-category identity with some clients, whom 'know' you within the context of a different role-category identity, is made recognisable. Therefore, we are provided with a series of utterances that make explicit the achieved nature of role-category identities as a members' concern within team meeting talk. Whilst the role-identity category in question is not being realised or interactionally carried out during the meeting, the practical accomplishment of allocating a role and discussing problems surrounding such an interactional strategy are discussed. Consequently, we may infer that role-category identities are the concern of members and the account suggests, that as a members phenomena, they are described in terms which make recognisable their occasioned and interactionally achieved sense *for members.*

Some Conversational Methods for Accomplishing 'Team Leadership'

The notion of Team Leadership is one that has been outlined in some detail, particularly with respect to some of the textual accounts of professional roles within a team. Essentially, the Team Leader is in charge of co-ordinating and allocating work to different members of the team. In terms of team meetings, it may be the Team Leader's role not only to 'chair' the proceedings, but also to co-ordinate the allocation of work, the exchange of information, inform members of the team the agenda for the day and deal with any problems between different members of the team. In many senses, the Team Leader role varies according to the type of team structure in operation. Despite the different models of team structure (Øvretveit 1994) the interactional establishment of leadership roles can be heard to be contingent on a number of interactive and conversational methods. In short, in terms of the local conversational machinery, the Team Leader 'role' can be heard to be grounded in the local specifics of turn-taking, category work and self-selection procedures identified by the work of conversation and membership categorisation analysts.

Within this extract the Team Leader is initiating a sequence within which he is attempting to canvass the views of the team members present about the proposal for establishing a community room. A community room can be understood as a place which members of the flood-hit community can use as a resource, alongside the team, in dealing with the effects of the flood (e.g. liasing with members of the flood-hit community and accessing relevant information, making phone calls etc).

Example Six – Team Meeting

```
1.TL:     Mmmm (.) asking for peoples opinions (.) does anyone have strong views
2.        on that? =
3.CDW:    = Well before you do its important to realise this is a final last ditch effort
4.        everything else fails we will be still busily running around trying to meet
5.        people (.)
6.TL:     Does anyone else have strong (.) views about the proposal then (.) do you
7.        think its a good idea or a bad idea or an indifferent idea? (.)
8.SW3:    I think its a good idea to have a room that the community could (.) use since
9.        your looking for somewhere (.) but since the move effects me =
10.TL:    = mmm[m  ]
11.SW3:        [I'm ] I'd want assurances that the room upstairs would be no
12.       smoking in my absence either (.)
13.TL:    mm yeh.
```

During the course of this extract, the TL asks for people to offer their opinions concerning the movement of people within the office space in order to make room for a community room that members of the community can use as a drop in centre. The TL does not make any explicitly recognisable reference to his role-identity category. However, he asks for other 'people's opinion' (L.1). In this sense, the TL selects other speakers to speak whilst not nominating anyone in particular, the CDW takes a turn that stresses the importance and validity of the proposed changes. This is followed by a long pause within which the TL self selects again in order to make a request for a fellow team member to make a further bid for the floor. The SW3 obliges by producing an utterance that describes the move and proposal as a 'good idea'. However, her utterance, 'but since the move effects me', elicits a prompting response by the TL. The SW3 then continues by referring to a need for 'assurances' concerning smoking in her absence from any new office space she would use. The TL makes an evaluative utterance in the form of a simple affirmation of the SW3's 'opinion talk' which then closes the sequence. Throughout this sequence, the TL has an array of speech rights that can be heard in terms of nominating potential speakers and dictating the flow of talk and the topic, this is not always the case in the transcribed data. However, the topic of changing rooms and the provision of a community room is a 'team matter'. Furthermore, as a team matter, the proposal has to be discussed by the team. This inference is supported by the TL's request for opinions. In this sense during the task of asking people for opinions (and the associated speech rights thereof) the TL displays a role-identity category incumbency that precludes the predicates of asking people for opinions during discussions concerning team issues (rather than client issues). Consequently, the recognisable work of doing Team Leadership and making it available to other team members can be heard to be contingent on conversational procedures. The prompting of the SW3's utterance reinforces the notion that members can offer opinions but not nominate others to speak or change topic at this stage. Furthermore, the evaluative utterance at the end of the sequence can be understood as part of an adjacency pair statement of *opinion / recognition of opinion*.

Within this extract the TL informs the Team that a new team member is arriving the following day. We can understand this in terms of the fact that the Team Leader, in terms of his category incumbency, is duty bound to refer to such changes in team membership.

Example Seven –Team Meeting

```
1.TL:    (X) starts tommorow (.) can we all give him a chance? (.)
2.LVC:   I'll give him a chance (.) I get on with him (X) he's okay
3.       (X) is
4.SW1:   Jus' cos he doesn't [ hold up your]
5.TL:                        [ remember   ] (X) is joining us rather
6.       than us joining him.
```

Within this stretch of talk the TL opens up a topic concerning the arrival of a new team member, the TL asks that he should be given 'a chance' (L.2). This is realised through the use of the 'we' pro-term, we may infer that this use of the term 'we' is significant in that not only does the Team Leader initiate a topic introducing the new team members imminent arrival but also uses the institutional 'we' category as a means of referring to a collective. In this case, the pro-term can be understood to refer to the 'collective/-institutional' category the of 'team'. The LVC responds to the open nomination of a turn on the floor by providing an utterance that ties the action-predicate of giving the new team member a chance with the phrase that he is 'okay' (L.2, 3), a descriptive predicate of 'personality' or 'character'. The SW1 responds to the LVC's statement by beginning to make an evaluation of the LVC's description of the new team member as 'okay' and that he is willing to give him a chance. However, the SW1 utterance (L.4) is interrupted by the TL who makes a recommendation that it should be remembered that the new team members is joining 'us' rather than 'us joining him' (L.5,6). The use of the term 'us', by the Team Leader, extends the use of pro-terms that act as descriptor terms for the collectivity being pointed to. In this case we may infer that the Team Leader is referring to 'the team'. Furthermore, he makes recognisable his role-identity category incumbency by displaying the warrantability of speaking on behalf and for the whole team and making recommendations for how the team should respond to the new arrival, his utterances are not contested in this respect.

The following extract displays the way in which the Team Leader initiates topics. Such topic initiation may be viewed as a predicated feature of the TL's (recognisable) interactionally displayed sense of incumbency. As such it provides a further example of the way, the methods, through which Team Leadership is achieved and made an accountable feature of the team meetings.

Example Eight – Team Meeting

1.TL: Right then gang (3.0) last week (1.0) look at the 17th of June (1.0) *****
2.   birthday on the sixteenth (.)
3.All: Yep.

During the course of this extract, the TL is requesting that Team members examine the calendar in order to assess the most suitable time for arranging the allocation of duties and work amongst team members during the week of the European elections. The TL asks the local 'gang' to examine specific dates. The request to examine the 17th of June is met by all the members responding with the term 'yep'. This is striking, in the sense that all team members are able to provide, in unison, an affirmative response to the TL's request. However, this is not just to do with good timing, but stems from the TL's use of the term 'gang' earlier in the sequence. It is through the use of this term that the TL makes recognisable that the talk is between him, the current speaker and the rest, as the 'gang'. The 'gang' therefore makes recognisable their understanding of what is being requested by the TL's talk. As I have stated, this reflects the recognisable role-identity incumbency of the TL that is interactionally and conversationally negotiated and accomplished *in situ*.

The following extract concerns the organisational particulars of returns (which document the referrals that member of the team may have carried out) and the organisational matters of 'keeping records'.

Example Nine – Allocation Meeting

1.SW1:   I haven't had a referral this month is that going to look bad on your
2.   returns?=
3.TL: = No =
4.SW1:   = Cos their not kept separate (.)
5.TL: They're not (.)
6.SW1:   As long as you are happy with that? (.)

7.TL: Yep (2.0)
8.   Any problems last week?

    Within this sequence, the talk concerns an organisational difficulty, namely the fact that the SW1 has not had a referral for 'this month' (L.1). The SW1 asks if 'that is going to look bad on your returns', the TL, recognising that this is a nomination for him to speak, says that it is not. The SW1 adds to her account of organisational difficulties by stating that the returns for the month are not 'kept separate' (L.4). The precise reading of this suggestion is not available, but we may surmise that returns are kept for the team as a whole, rather than for individual team members. An empty return for the month, for an individual team member could be, in organisational terms, problematic. This potential reading is displayed, in terms of the weak form of recognisability, by the design of the turn proffered by the SW1 which states the case (they're not kept separate) and can be heard as a request for an affirmation. The SW1 completes the sequence by stating 'as long as your happy with that' (L.5), the TL responds affirmatively. In this stretch of talk, the SW1's problem, and the design of the utterances aimed at the TL, display the role-identity category of the TL as recognisably oriented to by the SW1. The TL is in charge of referral returns and the organisational chapter work of the team as a whole. The TL, having answered the SW1's questions self selects a turn in order to introduce a 'touched off topic', namely whether any other team members had 'any problems last week'. Thus, the role-identity category of the TL is interactionally established through category work (problem talk and organisational difficulties) as well as the way in which the TL changes topic, answers questions and self selects a turn oriented to generating further utterances from other team members. Furthermore, the fact that records of the work carried out by team members is recorded in terms of a single overall document (namely the returns) provides a further method for the achievement of the team as a single, recognisable unit.
    In each of the examples examined I have sought to illustrate the way in which the role of the Team Leader is an oriented feature of the team meetings. Furthermore, this is displayed through the way in which the TL places himself within the local conversational environment and specific categories and predicates are tied to his incumbency. An additional method for achieving Team Leadership is the use of 'we' and 'us'. These terms are institutional devices *in the sense* that they stand on behalf of a collectivity, a device that includes all the members present, we may infer that this device is 'the team'. Furthermore, in terms of the locally established rules of conversation it is the Team Leader who not only changes topic by nominating other team members to speak but who also has specific rights over

recommendations, descriptions and suggestions for collective action as 'the team'.

Role as an Interactional/Organisational Device and Resource

In the following data extract members of the team are discussing changing the social geography of the office. Issues surrounding work, distractions, the division of labour, 'confidentiality' and the organisational order of the team are discussed. In other words, the office is to be rearranged in order that these considerations are dealt with. Additional issues, which are discussed by the team, involve the registration of the office (and its consequences) and a move to provide a community room that can be accessed by the flood hit community. The discussion raises a number of topics and issues that are heard to be connected with the proposals for the team's office.

Example Ten – Team Meeting

```
1.CDW: Cos there is (.) that's another decision but I'm specifically talking in terms
2.      of a registered office we can still use this as a registered office if your not
3.      into moving people around (.) it can still be done that way (.) if I'm only
4.      going to be using it two hours a day (.) what I was discussing with you is
5.      putting a proposal to the Team if push came to shove (.) it may well be that
6.      it is not (.) we don't have to do it (.) if you want to use another property and
7.      put that to community use (.) then then fine I (.)
8.TL:   I think it would be nice if there was a desk somewhere they can come
9.      around and use for the fax and photocopy [and ]
10.CDW:                                          [like ] your room would do =
11.TL:  = post recreation (.) translation
12.     (laughter)
13.LVC: And any other duties (.)
14.SW3: Well (name of TeamLeader) would not really be the best because he has to
15.     write the most important documents and he needs some peace and quiet to
16.     do it and if you were using his room you'd have anybody walking up past
17.     the other two rooms (.)
18.SW2: How (.) why didn't you agree with the suggestion that (name of CDW)
19.     stays down here (name of LVC) goes upstairs and we join (name of LVC)?
20.SW1: Well I just said that
21.LVC: Same principle (.) the suggestion that was made then
22.TL:  But there's quite a lot of confidential [things]
23.LVC:                                          [yeah ] social worker thing again see
24.     but still basically down to that (.) it is like (name of counsellor) when we
25.     started the beginning me and (name of Counsellor) shared a room in there it
26.     wouldn't (.) work now cos (name of Counsellor) files (.) (name of
27.     Counsellor) gone on with her job she's got stuff I am not allowed to see (.)
```

28.C: It worked fine when we (.)
29.LVC: Get ticking over =
30.C: = Reacting reacting to what was happening
31.LVC: Where as now (.) I couldn 't share a room with any of these because of
32.   what goes on (.) For example if they had a confidential phone call I'd have
33.   to walk out of the office while there going on the phone call (1.0) with three
34.   Social Workers (.) or whatever together (.) it doesn't matter does it cos they
35.   know about the allocations and what going on in each file =
36.SW1: = mmmm
37.CDW:I think the only fair thing you can do is wait until you have got a full team
38.   in.

In this extract, we can hear the topic to revolve around a change of purpose for part of the office and issues surrounding who occupies which part of the building. The CDW asserts that the establishment of a registered office may not involve changes, providing he is only there for two hours a day (L.1-6). A further suggestion proffered by the TL involves allocating some space for community use, the CDW suggests that the Team Leader's room would be used for such a venture. Clearly, the re-categorisation of the device 'office' as a 'registered office' and the associated predicate 'reorganising the location of Team members in the office' is mapped onto a secondary predicate, that is how much time the CDW spends at the office. This provides a further layer of category work, this can be heard in the way the re-organisation of the device 'office' to 'registered office' is also being tied to the predicated actions of the CDW. In this sense, the role-identity category of the CDW is being worked up and displayed in the course of the discussion. This is done through the identification of a category shift and the mapped predicates of time spent in the office and the device of 're-organisation' (which involves the predication of movement of Team members from their present location in the Office). The CDW responds to the TL statement that it would be 'nice' if a community room was provided.

We may infer that the category of 'space' is available in making sense of the device 're-organisation'. The suggestion, by the CDW that the TL's room would do as a community room, is met by an account by the SW3 that invokes specific predicates that are tied to the TL's role-identity category. Thus, the topic of the registered office and the community room is redirected towards a discussion concerning category incumbency. The SW3 argues that this is not feasible because the TL has to write some of the most important documents and 'needs some peace and quiet to do it'. We may hear this utterance as a set of predicates that can be praxiologically associated with the category incumbency of the TL. Furthermore, the SW3 states '...if you were using his room you'd have anybody walking past the other two rooms' (L.13-15). At this stage 'anybody' can be heard to apply to any member who does not fit into the same category/collection of which the role-identity category of the TL is a part. This could be heard as referring to the membership category 'professional team member' that the predicate of access to confidential information is a part. Furthermore, the reference to the 'other two' rooms can be heard as tying the category of location in the office space to a role-identity category, namely the category 'professional team members' of the device 'team member'.

The SW2 refers to a suggestion in which the LVC shares a room with the other social workers. We understand that this is the case due to the use of 'we', which is reflected in the recipient design of the next utterance by the SW1, who states that the suggestion was made earlier. In other words, this utterance displays which members hear the 'we', through the repair of the indexicality of 'we'. In this case the other social worker are tacitly displaying and hearing co-membership with SW3. However, the TL reiterates the earlier analysis proffered by the SW3 through the reference to the predicate of 'confidentiality' (L.20). The LVC agrees and then orients himself to the predicate of confidentiality (L.21-25, L.29-33) and displays how his category incumbency, if he was to be in proximity to the social workers, would result in him having to 'leave the room' if a 'confidential phone call' was underway.

Thus, the LVC exhibits how his membership of the category 'non-professional' of the device 'team member' would create a problem if this course of action was followed. This is reinforced by his reference to '...three social workers or whatever' who 'know' about 'allocations and what's going on in each file'. The predicates of different categories are therefore not only a topic of conversation but a resource through which the reorganisation of the office (as a meta-topic) is being discussed and constituted. Thus, the CDW, the LVC, the TL and the Social Workers can be heard to use category and predicate work in this way. Thus, 'rights and expectations' and demarcations between team members are made observable through the topic of registering the office and providing a community room. However, the CDW can be heard to be invoking a sense of incumbency through the mapping of predicates and the tying of 'registering the office' to the predicate of the amount of time he himself spends in the office. He initially uses the pro-term 'we' ('we can still use this as a registered office if you're not into moving people around'). However, he does some category shifting in the last utterance when he states '... I think the only fair thing you can do is wait until you've got a full team in' (L.35). Clearly, the use of the pro-term 'we' stands in contrast to the pro-term 'you'. The CDW shifts from the 'we' in the first utterance in this extract (... we don't have to do it) to 'you' in the last utterance in this extract. Therefore, we can hear how in the last utterance he displays his position, his role-identity incumbency in this instance, as outside the team. Presumably, this also means that the registration of the office, which he ties to his category (of role-identity) incumbency, also stands outside the team and seems to be tied to his incumbent position.

Therefore, in this extract we can hear how the use of references to membership categories and their associated predicates are not only being interactionally accomplished, but also being deployed as a means of making a decision. Therefore, to this extent we may see how references to such 'documents' is also a conversationally strategic device that is being deployed in and through the endogenous accomplishment of order. Furthermore, we can see how different accomplishments and descriptions of role-identity categories, in this instance, provide for a range of different competencies and duties within the 'multidisciplinary team'. Confidential information can only be shared with certain team members and the position of the Team Leader is described as 'important work' which requires peace and quiet. The discussion concerning the movement of personnel and the 'working geography' of the Flood Support Teams office space provides a vehicle for these distinctions to be displayed and reflexively oriented to within this instance of team interaction.

Conclusion

During the course of this chapter I have sought to illustrate, through reference to transcribed material, some interactional dimensions of role within multidisciplinary team talk. Whilst these analyses are confined to specific locally situated instances a number of observations can be made. Firstly, that within the course of team meetings role is both interactionally accomplished and recognised and used as a resource to carry out further work in meeting talk. Team members negotiate and contest role through the recognisable deployment of a range of finely ordered and masterful techniques and strategies. Role is not imposed from above but is an emergent property of team members work within meetings. In this sense therefore, the respecification of role as a locally ordered and interactionally achieved device seems, in terms of the examples and analysis carried out above, reasonable. Furthermore, the way in which members reflexively monitor and use role as a resource to make decisions (e.g. arranging office space), close down accounts, downgrade or recognise other team members contributions provides for a view of team membership as an activity that utilises a range of skills, methods and strategies which are necessary for accomplishing the context of the meetings and carrying out the business of such meetings. The local specifics of members work is in contrast to the descriptions and outlines of multidisciplinary teamwork described in social/care management based literature. The appreciation of such observed practices may be of use to those interested in exploring such sites or work within similar contexts. Therefore, this chapter does not seek to criticise theoretical accounts of role. Rather it aims to provide a detailed conversation and membership categorisation analytic study of the fine detail of interaction within a multidisciplinary meeting. Consequently, the model of role evident within literature concerned with multidisciplinarity and teamwork outlined and discussed earlier in this book (e.g. Øvretveit 1994) could benefit from the consideration of role as an interactional device and *resource* that is reflexively oriented to, accomplished, contested, negotiated and deployed during the course of the everyday work of team members in meetings.

The following chapter explores further examples of talk-in-interaction as a means of investigating the situated characteristics and interactional parameters of displaying knowledge within multidisciplinary contexts. Again, as discussed during the concluding part of chapter one, knowledge (along with role and communicative practice and interactional structure) is central to the theorised models of multidisciplinary teamwork that are an important consideration in this study. It is to the social organisation and display of knowledge within the multidisciplinary setting examined that I now turn.

Note

1   For a more sequential account of role-in-interaction an account by Whalen and Zimmerman (1990) is particularly good. Through the examination of citizens calls to the police they show how the category entitlements of actors inform and mutually elaborate upon the sense of members accounts of events.

5 Knowledge and Display in Team Meetings

Introduction

Conversation Analysis can be understood to be primarily interested in sequences in talk. However, the early work of Harvey Sacks also displayed a concern with categories, talk and interaction. Levinson (1994) notes how members' talk can be understood as an interactional management system within which categories in talk are sequentially managed through turn taking, extended sequences recipient design and so forth. Levinson also notes how the analysis of talk-in-interaction is understood both in terms of the paradigmatic (categorial) and syntagmatic (sequential) dimensions of conversation. However, I do not wish to pursue Levinson's observation at this stage *per se*. Rather I wish to explore the approach of Membership Categorisation Analysis (as it relates to analysing knowledge-in-interaction), recent developments within this methodological approach and outline the concern with both sequence and category that will inform my analysis of knowledge and knowledgeability in multidisciplinary team meetings. It is my assumption that the interactional dimensions of knowledge in terms of talk-in-interaction within 'meetings' demands a concern with categories (Atkinson, Cuff and Lee 1978), turn taking (Sacks, Schegloff and Jefferson 1974), topic organisation (Sacks 1992 a,b, Coulthard 1977) and the sequential downgrading and upgrading of utterances in members' praise recognition work (Pomerantz 1978).

Multidisciplinary Team Work and Knowledge

Within the confines of multidisciplinary teamwork the theoretical and academic literature surrounding such formal interactive structures implicitly perceives such contexts as a means by which different members of the team provide qualitatively distinct types of expertise, knowledge and 'know-how'. The display of 'know-how' and knowledge is of fundamental theoretic import to conceptualisations of 'effective multidisciplinary teamwork'.[1] The notion of different types of 'specialist knowledge' filtering in to the decision making process provides for a mass model of exponentially improving levels of expertise and a belief in canvassing as many opinions as possible in deciding and pursuing particular courses of action. Furthermore, such an approach is viewed as a means of optimising the efficiency of decision making and meeting clients needs in a more holistic fashion. For example, within literature concerning multidisciplinary team practice the team (and the different roles within the team) is viewed as the vehicle through which different bodies of expertise and knowledge are transmitted. As Øvretveit (1994:55) states:

> ... the term 'team' is used to refer to a multidisciplinary team. It emphasises two features of these teams. First, the importance of relationships to the purpose of the group: relationships both between a client and a team member, and between members and each other. these relationships are not secondary to the goal of the team, as they are in some project teams in industry, but are the means through which these relationships are different in different types of team. The second feature is that the combination of team members' efforts is greater than the sum of each person's contribution. A team is a way of co-ordinating each person's efforts so that the final result is of a different order than the sum of each person's efforts.

Evers (1981:209) argues that multidisciplinary teamwork provides a framework through which the expertise, information and knowledge of individual members can be fed into the (ideally) collaborative multidisciplinary decision making process through the activities of :

> ... mutual accommodation and exchange of information amongst a company of equals, each contributing on the basis of their authoritative knowledge and expertise...

These views of knowledge and expertise in multidisciplinary team interaction and practice are echoed by a number of other social/care work commentators (Belbin, 1981; Guzzo and Shea, 1992; West, 1994). In this chapter, I will seek to contrast this conceptualisation of knowledge and team structure with the thick description of some examples of members' practices within a multidisciplinary team site using ethnomethodological oriented approaches to knowledge, knowhow, expertise and consider the relationship between categories, knowledge and talk. It is to these considerations that we now turn.

Lexical Choice and Category Display

The notion of lexical choice[2] attempts to describe the display of different vocabularies and categories within specific contexts. Furthermore, it is a notion that provides an avenue for reconciling the concerns of category analysis and the sequential organisation of talk. Drew and Heritage (1992:29) during the course of their introductory chapter state:

> Lexical Choice is a significant way through which speakers evoke and orient to the institutional context of their talk. Numerous studies have documented the incidence of 'lay' and 'technical' vocabularies in such areas as talk and medicine, and it is clear that the use of such vocabularies can embody definite claims to specialised knowledge and institutional identities.

They continue by arguing that such choices are context sensitive and are displayed and oriented to the practical accomplishment at hand. Furthermore, Van Dijk (1997) notes how institutional contexts may also be characterised by the display of specific grammatical forms, turn-taking systems, person references and institutionally specific references. At first glance this concept can be considered as a useful framework for exploring the relationship between knowledge, talk and interaction. However, the notion is not without some inherent tensions between the *in situ* characteristics of members' work and the desire to relate practical action to the formal descriptions and understandings of institutions and organisations. The notion of lexical choice suggests that interlocutors choose utterances which are representative of a lexicon of words, technical vocabularies or 'knowledge' (i.e. a set of pre-existing categorial orders) that can be readily described as professional, medical or 'lay'. However, whilst not rejecting the concept of lexical choice, in this chapter I seek to focus how the display of categories in 'utterances' are heard as 'knowledgeable' in terms of the *local management of talk* deployed during the course of a meeting. In order to develop this ethnomethodological focus during my analysis of knowledge, talk and interaction in multidisciplinary team meetings a consideration of a seminal piece of work on knowledge, knowhow and ethnomethodology will be considered. I will then proceed by providing a brief description of the team observed during the research that informs this work and the analysis of the transcribed data utilising the principles derived from recent developments within Membership Categorisation Analysis.

Ethnomethodology and Knowledge

From an ethnomethodological point of view, knowledge is both grounded in terms of members' practical reasoning and realised as a locally produced feature of members' work. Stoddart's (1974) work on herion users 'argot' and Sharrock's (1974) piece *On Owning Knowledge* are relevant to this set of ideas. This is due to the manner through which these studies pay attention to and illustrate the situated accomplishment of knowledge as a practical activity that is grounded in members' mundane practices. I will focus on Sharrock's work as a means of describing and explicating the main characteristics of the ethnomethodological position as they relate to this chapter.

Within traditional sociological enquiry the relationship between society's members and wider bodies of knowledge is a problematic one. Sharrock (1974:45) notes the way in which notions such as 'culture', 'perspective', 'ideology' and 'world view' are used as a means of explaining the activities of members and an assumed external body of knowledge. In the case of multidisciplinary team meetings a similar question emerges. How can the activities of different team members within multidisciplinary meetings be understood in terms of wider, distinct knowledge bases? Whilst this reformulation of the question does not relate to social structure *per se* it does relate to the fundamental issue of relating structure (in the form of some of the descriptions of multidisciplinary team work referred to in this chapter) to members' activities. Sharrock (1974:45) characterises this *issue* thus:

> To suppose that a connection can be made between a collectivity's corpus and its members' activities is to presuppose that there is already such a relationship between the corpus of knowledge and the social structure as will permit the ascription of the corpus to one or another activity.

Sharrock notes how the understanding, identification and description of knowledge and its ascription to a range of activities trades on the commonsensical sense making methods of ordinary members of society. Furthermore, he describes the way in which traditional modes of social scientific practice describe members' practices as constituting a corpus of knowledge that the members of the ascribed group may not necessarily identify with (1974:50). This leads us to the question: to what extent do different team members of a multidisciplinary team represent, through their activities within multidisciplinary team meetings, different corpuses of knowledge? Indeed to what extent can we talk of team members connecting with external bodies of knowledge? From an ethnomethodological point of view this question needs to be respecified in terms of how practices and activities constitute knowledge within multidisciplinary team meetings. In what follows, I will focus on multidisciplinary meetings as sites where knowledge is displayed. I will do this by focussing on the categories displayed and oriented to through the sequential organisation of talk within the formal framework of the meeting using the principles, concepts and analytical framework discussed and described during the previous stages of this chapter.

Analysis

The following extract occurs at the beginning of a team meeting that has been transcribed using notation derived from the work of Gail Jefferson (1978).[3] It concerns an utterance that involves the elicitation of 'detail' about a specific client. The discussion is concerned with different team members' contact with a particular client. Within the context of supporting flood victims different members of the Flood Support Team would often have contact with the same people, albeit in different capacities.

Example One – Team Meeting

1.TL: They should be contacted soon then ? (3.0)
2.   (Indistinguishable chatter)
3.LVC: Oh that's Mrs ***** for you though (.) the one we are dealing with (.)
4.   lives on Queens road (.) we love the old lady (.) that's her sister who lives
5.   on X road (.) now then when she was flooded we had to take it to her
6.   sisters first (.) unload it there (.) unload it there then let her sister check it
7.   first then get her sister around Y place (.)
8.SW1:   [You have qualifications for this then]
9.LVC: [Her older sister said yes the other one] was allowed to have the furniture
10.   (2.0) so then we took it around to Mrs *****.

The data extract involves a conversational display by the lay volunteer co-ordinator. In one sense, the topic is touched off from the initial utterance that refers to contacting a specific client. The LVC's turn can be heard as a method of 'self-selection' (L.3) and he produces an account that resembles the Sacksian description of the story format. The story preface is designed in terms of the previous utterance and we are presented with a matrix of identifier predicates. These consist of the predicate of being, the predicate of the client being dealt with by the lay volunteers, the predicate of where she lives, the predicate of the emotional attachment displayed by certain members of the team to the client in question and finally the geographical location of an immediate member of the client's family (L.3. L.4). Thus, the five predicates serve to locate the client and identify the client in a number of different ways. However, together they form a preface that displays a particular familiarity or knowledge of the client in question. Furthermore, they serve to preface a story and demonstrate a form of knowledgeability that not everyone holds. This sequence is followed by what Sacks calls the 'story proper' and in many respects the preface prepares the listeners for the newsworthy item (L.5-9). In terms of topical coherence, it involves a story concerning the relationship between the client, her sister, the volunteers and the removal of furniture. Furthermore, the account involves invoking the predicate of 'checking' that is tied to the category sister. The category of 'sister' as a membership category of 'family' is tied to a further type of process predicate[4] of warrantability, namely the sister 'allowing' furniture (a device of the collection *objects to be moved*) to be transported to the client's residence. The conclusion of the account is enunciated in a form that acknowledges and reflexively reaffirms the sequential organisation of the category coherence of the topic in question. That is to say, at the point of having conversationally reached the predicates of 'checking' and 'allowing' by a family member, the course of action was completed and the story is closed.

The organisation of the category flow and the methods of categorisation work evident in this extract exhibit the provision of information within the parameters of category incumbency. The role-identity of the interlocutor (as an interactionally accomplished, available and recognisable category of membership) is brought to bear on the conversational interaction. This statement or inference may appear to be relying on ethnographic knowledge of who is speaking (e.g. the lay volunteer co-ordinator) which is incorporated into the notational structure of the transcripts. This criticism of the Institutional Talk Program (Drew and Heritage 1992) and Levinson's use of such information in inferring the social inter-subjectivity of lexically organised utterances (Levinson 1992) is one that should be noted (Watson 1997). However, I wish to consider the Sacksian notion of recognisability, as a members' phenomena, as a way of illustrating, locating and describing the contextual details of *methods* by which recognisable differences in category flow (and hence the intelligibility of different types of knowledge, 'know-how' and opinion) are accomplished. Furthermore, the relationship between a given category incumbency and the conversational display of relevant categories of knowledge etc. will be explored.

One way of attempting this type of analysis is to consider the extract in terms of the recognisability and availability of such category work for members. That is to say, within the activity of the team meeting the role-identity of another team member may be taken up as a topic at any given time. It is an omni-relevant topic (generated by the meta-device of 'the meeting)' insofar as the device 'meeting', categories of meeting and modes of predication (talking, discussing, representing a position or role within a meeting or a particular perspective etc) are members' phenomena. Despite the fact that team-members do not always make explicit references to questions of role-identity category incumbency and warrantability[5], the availability of such categorisations in talk *informs* the interaction within the team in recognisable ways. In one sense, it can be construed as a reflexive arc within which recognisability organises *both* the sequential and categorial features of talk. It is a reflexive arc in that both local historical factors (diachrony in Sassurian terms) and the possibility of what is going to be said (the future) inform the dynamic achievement of synchrony as an ongoing interactional discursive process. The availability of what *can be* categorised and the recipient contingency of what *is being* categorised inform the here and now in an ongoing 'no time out' process. To this extent the personal categories of role-identity within the team can be understood as an 'interactional device', as opposed to the functionalist and static conceptualisation of role as a structurally generated social script (a conceptualisation that remains intact within social/care work literature e.g. Øvretveit 1994). We can also understand role as a device that members may use and deploy within local settings and activities. As Halkowski (1990: 565) notes:

> Rather than treating "role" as a self evident, social scientific resource for analysis, and following the work of Garfinkel (1967) and Zimmerman and Pollner (1970) social scientists should take it as a topic of study. Doing so will help illuminate how interactants organise the social world by their use of these conceptions and actions.

An example of some of the analytical points mentioned above involves the reference to 'qualifications' by SW1 (L.7) (as a predicate of the device 'professionals'). This can be understood as a method for drawing our attention to a problematic reading of the LVC's account. This is achieved by invoking predicates associated with the role identity category incumbency and warrantability of the speaker, i.e. the lay volunteer co-ordinator. That is to say, the display of information or 'know-how' within the conversational structure of the story is questioned in terms of the role-category incumbency and warrantability of who is speaking. The role-category incumbency of the lay volunteer co-ordinator and issues surrounding his category display can therefore be seen as members' phenomena. His display of knowledge, of familiarity with a client, her predicament and the course of action carried out are questioned in terms of a method of mapping his available role-category incumbency (as an available and locally occassioned device) to the predicate of being non-qualified (L.7). Therefore this conversational interaction displays the way in which categories of role-identity can inform conversational procedures and display the warrantability (legitimacy) or unwarrantability (illegitimacy) of what is being said within the team based setting.

Displaying Knowledge-in-talk

Further examples of category display can be seen within other contexts. In the following example a discussion concerning the arrangement of a drop in centre is of topical interest. The talk involves a discussion concerning the relationship between the proposed opening times of the drop in centre and categories of different types of people who might wish to use such a facility.

Example Two – Team Meeting

1.C:	He he so er Mrs Jones pointed at my Case work (.) they are setting up
2.	their own drop in (.) every Friday (1.0) from ten till twelve
3.	(indistinguishable)
4.SW1:	Why can't we do two till five or =
5.TL:	= Can't we have the community centre two till five (.)
6.SW1:	Could get another place ? =
7.St.:	= most people want to go home (.)
8.C:	A lot of people picking up children and stuff
9.SW2:	Yes
10.SW3:	But if you are going to (.) pick children up (.) it's a better time particularly
11.	if it's raining (.) what do you want to do arrange a rota now? (1.5)
12.C:	We are going to need to (1.5) cos (name of colleague) will be off next
13.	week (.)
14.TL:	I should have thought ten till two (1.5) having people around =
15.SW3:	= Rather than relying on phones etc (.)
16.TL:	Hmm [mm]
17.SW1:	[We're] putting them in a category aren't we a number of the
18.	population don't have school children (1.5) or children they have at home
19.	all day anyway (.)because it is believed (.) that people in their twenties
20.	and thirties are actually going to be depriving everyone else (1.5)
21.TL:	Well were doing the help line (1.0) can't do everything =
22.SW3:	= We're going to be pretty spread out aren't we?

During the course of this extract the topic of providing a 'drop in centre' for the flood-hit community is discussed. Topics surrounding categories of time, place and finally people are brought to bear on the conversation. The categories of 'time and place' are used as relevant criteria in scheduling the proposed 'drop in' service to clients in the flood-hit community. Issues surrounding time and place are raised initially by SW1 who suggests a specific time namely 'two till five...' (L.4). However, one of the places where the drop in can be held (the community centre) is not available at this time. This leads to the suggestion by SW1 that another place for the 'drop in' service could be found (L.6). However, both the student and the counsellor raise issues or topics concerning the activities of people and times of day, in this case people picking children up from school (L.8, 9). Picking children up from school can be heard to be a consistent predicate of the membership category 'people' but not necessarily a universal attribute of the whole population.

This talk is followed by further exchanges concerning the formal organisation of the times for the drop in centre (L.10. L.11), the undesirability of leaving such arrangements to the last minute and contacting team members by phone if and when they are required. This is then followed by an account from SW1 who refers to a problem contained in the decisions made during the previous talk. The account begins with the use of the pro-term 'we' which can be heard to invoke the institutional device of the team. However, the account may also be heard to refer to professionals in the team, as they are the only members who have spoken at this stage. The lack of judgement or problem identified by SW1 is one of tying the device 'people' to a uniform set of predicates. As has been stated, SW1 opens by co-selecting the device 'people', proffered by the team leader at L.13, in response to the counsellor's and student's account, with the device 'population'. However, the device of population is then used as a resource for introducing the reference to a 'number of the population' either having school children or not having school children. Thus, in succinct terms the tying of the universal devices of people and population to predicates of behaviour within times of the day is transformed through the deployment of further membership categories associated with the device. These associated categories, in turn, make available different predications and attributes of behavioural patterns and/or lifestyles than those implied by the first form of categorisation. Thus, we can see how the topic is managed and transformed, not just through turn-taking but through the mutually elaborative and situated category work of team members.

In more detailed terms, the talk can be viewed in the following way. SW1 (L.4) is making a bid for the floor in order to confront the initial account. The explanation of a lack of judgement is pursued through the deployment of further categorisation work. The newsworthy item of SW1's account (L.16) is the misrepresentative nature of the category display proffered by the counsellor and the student. The reference to people in their 'twenties and thirties' (L.18), a further membership category of the general device 'population', is qualified by the display of specific predicate work. In this case, it is believed that this category of the population is in the least need of support as opposed to the primacy attached to the category of human organisation known as 'the family' within the community. We may argue that a particular view of the delivery of services and care is being displayed by SW1 here in a fashion which is both reflexive, analytical and designed in terms of the recognisable features of a claim to expertise, namely the expertise or the knowledge that a social worker can be commonsensically understood to possess.

In completing the story, the responses by the Team Leader (L.20) and SW3 (L.21) are relevant. References to doing other things, the inability to do everything and being 'pretty spread out' are hearable predicates that invoke a relational pair of 'time and resources'. Whilst they are not explicitly uttered, the predicates of 'depriving other people', which in terms of recipient design is constructed in terms of the preceding talk, allow the categories of both 'time' and 'resources' to be made available. It is this 'availability' achieved through category predicate work that provides for the references to 'being pretty spread out' by SW3 at the close of the extract (L.21).

Such a secondary account by SW1 can be seen to contest the initial view proffered at the beginning of the extract. The tying of the category 'people', as a response to the initial view proffered by SW1, to the category 'population' allows for a particular category display (e.g. different types of people and lifestyles). This particular category of the population is displayed through the insertion of the reference to the belief that a certain category of the population are 'depriving everyone else' of scarce resources and services offered by the drop in centre (i.e. people in their twenties and thirties who don't have families). However, through the method of availability (for this is a member's method insofar as it is interactionally, conversationally and praxiologically accomplished) the categories of 'time and resources' are made available as a means of closing and making sense of the conversation. The moral category of depriving people is negated by the organisational category of time and resources through category shifting in the next turn taken. This example illustrates the way in which category display, and the warrantable features of interactionally achieved role-identity incumbency, provide for the means through which 'knowledgeable' accounts are displayed. However, in order for such organised categorial schema to be understood as knowledgeable, such accounts are routinely and reflexively tied to the ongoing local accomplishment of interlocutors, various senses of role-identity (category) incumbency.

In the following part of this chapter the methods through which various accounts are interactionally recognised as knowledgeable will be explored. This will involve an examination of the precise recognition work that team members use during the course of some instances of the meetings examined during the study.

Recognising Utterances as Knowledgeable

In the following extract the talk involves a discussion concerning a client, the Team Leader and other team members who are familiar with the case. However, within this talk SW2 is invited to provide an account, within which a more detailed story emerges, to which the Team Leader responds: the exchange of information in this way was a feature of the allocation meetings transcribed. One possible reason for this was because the discussion of clients at such meetings could take on a more elaborate form. This can be understood in terms of the fact that the Team members present at allocation meetings were all accountable to professional modes of conduct and confidentiality, as well as being responsible for the statutory aspects of the Team caseload. Therefore, discussions could include more detailed information about flood victims.

Example Three – Allocation Meeting

1.SW1: Margaret needed (1.0) I spoke to her for sometime on the phone
2.TL: She's the (name of Village) one
3.SW1: What is she (1.0) what is this about her =
4.SW2: = She's she 's o::ne of those who were flooded in (name of the village)
5.   and she's feeling tearful and generally (1.0) she's got (.) she wanted to
6.   know who to contact to get her washing machine (1.0) condemned by
7.   environmental health (.) but she carried on and on talking and so I came to
8.   an arrangement (1.0) with her (.)
9.TL: Was there any response from the counsellor?

In this allocation meeting the social worker (SW2) provides an account of a client during which we are told that she is 'feeling tearful' (L.4, 5), a predicate of the device 'state of mind'. SW2 refers to 'problems' and 'troubles' which include the condemnation of her washing machine by environmental health and problems knowing 'who to contact' (L.5) to help her with the predicament. SW2 (L.7) then closes the account by stating that she took a course of action, namely the making of an 'arrangement', presumably to deal with these 'problems and troubles'. The TL responds to the story by asking, 'was there any response from the counsellor? ' (L.8). In terms of recipient design, the TL's talk is designed in terms of the predicate of feeling 'tearful' and the associated device of *state of mind*. Consequently, the utterance is dealt with as a document that the counsellor may have responded to or indeed may need to respond to. Thus, the account, as 'reportage', is made recognisable and the reference to any response from the counsellor suggests that she may be able to address the clients' predicament reported in the account. Furthermore, the first part of the story that connects the client with the category 'flood victim', is then mapped to the predicate of 'feeling tearful'. This provides a device through which a response from the counsellor may be viewed as an expected next part. In this sense, not only do we hear the recognisable display of an account as an informed piece of reportage due to the way other team members do not question SW2's observations and account of the client, it also makes available the types of categories and modes of predication that clients may be reported to possess as a praxiological and recognisable domain for a response by the counsellor. Thus, the knowledgeability of counselling is made available in and through the TL's response and recipient design. Furthermore, through the use of the strong form of recognisability the account is seen as containing problems and troubles which the 'counsellor' (i.e. someone who has the knowledge to deal with internal states of mind, feelings and emotions) can deal with. Having examined the manner through which utterrances are interactionally recognised as knowledgeable (and therefore managed as such) I will now seek to examine an instance of talk in interaction within which the knowledgeable status of utterances is an overt and *contested* topic for members of the flood support team.

Knowledge and Validity as a Member's Phenomenon

The following extract involves a discussion concerning the details of a child care order and the actions of the local social services authority. The discussion involves an exchange of views on the dimensions of carrying out child care orders (on children who may be deemed to be at risk by professionals) and the child care policy that the local social service department is pursuing. This is an important discussion for the professional members of the flood support team as it provides them with an opportunity to assess and exchange views on wider aspects of the working environment and the precise details of specialised areas of care that some team members are more familiar with.

Example Four – Allocation Meeting

1.SW1: I think this should go to someone more experienced in child care (.)
2.TL: Sounds almost like are:as got itself into a bit of a hole =
3.SW1: = I don't think they think like that (.) I think they feel it was alright and
4.   they knew from Y (.) the support worker things were not that bad
5.St::   How can you (.)
6.SW1: Well you know in the scale of priorities in child care this is probably quite
7.   low (.)
8.SW2: No not if (.) it's on a care order because they can actually be held (.) it can
9.   be a load of trouble (.) I'm surprised =
10.SW1:   = Well its their policy (.)
11.SW2:I really am (.) I thin[:k]
12.TL: [It] needs some discussion...

Within this stretch of talk a discussion concerning a specific referral is being conducted. SW1 states that someone who is more 'experienced in child care' should take the referral. Clearly, supervising childcare is seen to require 'experience' (L.1). The TL responds to the opinion proffered by referring to 'area' getting 'into a bit of a hole' (L.2). We hear 'area' as referring to a category of official social service organisation and the mapped predicate (a metaphor in this case) referring to the category of organisation making decisions that have created difficulties. SW1 (L. 3,4) responds to this recipiently designed turn by disagreeing with the TL's additional analysis of SW1's initial utterance. The category of social service organisation, namely the category 'area', is transformed to the pro-term 'they'. This is followed by the tying of the category to the predicate of knowing from the initial person involved with the case (the support worker) that 'things were not that bad' (L.4). The use of the pro-term 'they' can be heard to be a construction that ascribes the commonsensical parameters of personal characteristics to an organisational category. The notion that area can 'think' or 'know' is constituted through the use of 'they'. As a pro-term it helps the following predicates, which are tied with the category 'area', make sense, more feasible and praxiologically acceptable. During this point of the talk the student who asks a question (L.5) interrupts the two-party exchange between SW1 and the TL. The question is, in terms of the strong form of recognisability, an ethno-epistemological topic that is made conversationally available. It can be described in this way because the student topicalises the knowledgeability of the utterance in terms of a question which concerns the validity, legitimacy and 'truth' of SW1's account. The student asks how SW1 'knows' that their proffered account is valid. SW1 uses personal predicates of thought in proffering the opinion to which the student refers to, notably the use of the term, 'I think they feel it was alright... .' In one sense the phrase 'How do you know' reflects SW1's use of the term 'I think... .' The validating claim in SW1's utterance can therefore be heard to be questioned. The use of the term, 'I think', is pointed to (conversationally) by the student as part of the design of the claim that is being questioned. This is made recognisable by the way the utterance 'How do you know' stands adjacent to the previous utterance; and is recipiently designed in response to the personal modes of predication and validation proffered by SW1. The adjacency can be observed not just in sequential terms but also in terms of membership categorisation. SW1's reference to 'they' (L.3) is mirrored by the use of the pro-term 'you' by the student.

SW1 responds by beginning with the statement 'well you know' (L.6). This can be understood as a preface for what follows next. SW1 refers to the 'scale of priorities in child care' which in this particular instance is seen to be at the lower end of the conversationally referred to 'scale'. SW1 can be heard to revalidate the questioned account through a situated 'switch' of the categories displayed. This is done through reference to categories associated with the everyday professional work of social work practice. Although it is not recognisably explicit, the preface seems to suggest that the student should know about the professional particulars that SW1 is referring to. However, despite this revalidating strategy, SW2 questions SW1's new set of claims (L.7, 8). SW2 orients this questioning to the categories displayed by SW1. Thus, the reference to 'care orders' can be heard to be conversationally tied, recipiently designed, in terms of 'child care' and 'care orders' and the associated predicates of 'the scale of priorities'. In both cases the categories of 'child care' and 'care orders' can, when heard together, be heard to be categories of the device 'child protection'. SW2's objection to SW1's set of claims centres on the modes of predication derived from the device 'care order'. This, we are told, could mean 'loads of trouble' (L.8), which we understand as being tied not only to the category of a 'care order' but also the 'area', the local social services organisation, the *'they'* of SW1's second utterance in this stretch of talk. This is reaffirmed by SW1's response, 'well it's their policy' (L. 9). The TL closes this stretch of talk by recognising, and making recognisable, that different 'professional claims' are being displayed (L. 11). This is achieved through the reference, by the TL, for a need to discuss the matter. The use of the predicate 'discussion' makes available the categories of different professional claims in terms of the weak form of recognisability. In other words while such a set of categories are not explicitly referred to the provision of a predicate (namely the activity of discussing) provides the availability of such category displays to be an oriented feature of the members' talk.

This stretch of talk exhibits the way in which questions surrounding the validity of knowledge can be members' topics in their own right. Questions surrounding how and why members know what they know are clearly observable and available in the data examined. In this case, SW1 attempted to deploy professional categories to revalidate her initial, questioned claim. In this sense, the method of 'knowledge as category display' was used as a means of validating the claim. This is important, as it shows that knowledgeability is not merely an analytical or theoretical description, rather, it suggests that in and through conversational activity the method of knowledgeability is one which is not only 'understood' but also conversationally oriented to as *a strategy for making claims* and ensuring that a claim is heard as 'valid'.

Conclusion

During the course of this chapter I have sought to examine how knowledge and the display of knowledge are situated products of interactional and conversational work. Thus the notion that team members occupy clearly defined positions which have an intimate and direct relationship with exterior bodies of knowledge is eschewed. The model of multidisciplinarity as a framework through which distinct bodies of knowledge feed into decision making through a team framework, needs to be considered alongside the *in situ* interactional characteristics of the exchange of information and the recognition of knowledgeable utterances within team based contexts. Clearly, this study examines instances and extracts of the talk within the meetings examined and not a wide data set of examples. However, I have sought to show how interactionally accomplished senses of incumbency and the categorial and sequential methods of recognition work are of fundamental import to the conversational display of knowledge in team meetings. Indeed, the principle of knowledge being a situated phenomenon is one which considerations of meeting talk and those interested in promoting dialogue and the exchange of information between team members or individuals within groups should consider. Furthermore, during the course of this chapter some methods through which the situated character of knowledge is accomplished have been examined. These include sequential methods of organising and managing talk and the display of categories in conversation. The accountable and recognisable features of members' design of talk and the situated mechanism of turn-taking have a direct relationship with the production and recognition of team members' utterances. Team members do not only follow configurations of adjacency during turn taking but also attend to the category display (i.e. topic) being managed. Consequently, the mechanisms by which certain utterances are recognised as opposed to others and the means through which speech rights are managed are of epistemological importance through their reflexive and praxiological relationship with the various topics and decisions of team meetings. Therefore a view of knowledge as a detached and transcendental phenomenon is respecified in terms of the detailed and *methodic* interactional and discursive work of team members.

Notes

1   As in Øvretveit (1994).
2   As described by Levinson in Pragmatics (1994). Levinson utilises the concept as a means of beginning to reconcile conversation analysis with other developments within Pragmatics. In particular, he deploys it as a means of addressing the scant attention paid by sequential analyses of talk to the role of categories in talk.
3   The term 'process predicate' refers to utterances in which predicate groups can be heard to do a particular job e.g. identifying people, describing colour or mental state. However, I wish to emphasise that such groups or sets of process predicate are locally produced and designed in terms of local contingencies.
4   This term refers to the adequate connection between a specific membership category and a set of predicates of rights, entitlements, abilities and in this case informed understanding of the tasks at hand.

6 Narrative, Extended Sequences and Talking Team Work

During the course of this chapter I intend to examine the use of story formats in team talk-in-interaction. Øvretveit (1994) has identified the exchange of information, meaning and dialogue as one of the central features of effective team practice. Indeed, within the context of team work and community care, little research has been carried out into the precise dimensions of this requirement. This chapter aims to describe and empirically illustrate a potential line of development for research in this area. However, before outlining the methodological approach deployed in this chapter and presenting an analysis of the transcribed materials gathered from the aforementioned research project a consideration of the topic of narrative and stories within talk-in-interaction will be provided.

Analysing Stories and Narratives in Qualitative Research

The occurrence of stories within interview data has been well documented (Cortazzi 1993 and Coffey and Atkinson 1996). Furthermore, anthropological work (e.g. Preston 1978 and Toelken 1975) have illustrated how stories express cultural categories, facilitate the sharing of individual experiences and function to maintain and reproduce the normative and cultural organisation of the group. Coffey and Atkinson (1996:54) argue that stories can be understood in terms of both structure (i.e. stories have a beginning, middle and end) and function (i.e. a stories are deployed by members in order to achieve a goal). Coffey and Atkinson (1996:62) note that stories may be understood in terms of their form and considered in terms of their situated production. They state:

> The analysis of narratives can also focus on the social action implied in the text. This can involve taking a slightly less systematic and structured approach to narrative analysis, deriving more context-dependent infrastructure and focus to explain the effect (intended or unintended, implicit or explicit) of the story or tale. This emphasises the idea that

individual narratives are situated within particular interactions and within specific social, cultural, and institutional discourses.

Coffey and Atkinson (1996:76) continue by referring to ethnopoetics and describe the extent to which stories occur in everyday life. Furthermore, ethnopoetics is viewed a way of referring to the way in which members provide oral performances in a variety of social settings. Bauman (1986:3 in Coffey and Atkinson 1996:76) states that stories can be understood as:

> ... a mode of communication, a way of speaking, the essence of which resides in the assumption of responsibility to an audience for a display of communicative skill, highlighting the way in which communication is carried out, above and beyond its referential content.

Whilst these authors clearly appreciate the situated character of story production, the precise characteristics of situated talk (as opposed to interview data) and the means of analysing these characteristics is not attended to. Ethnomethodology and conversation analysis, on the other hand, have produced a range of studies and corpus of empirical work that has investigated the situated character of members' talk and 'narrative'. It is to this approach to the analysis of stories and talk-in-interaction that I now turn.

Stories, Accounts and Extended Sequences in Team Meetings

As has been outlined, an important feature of members' talk is the conversational structure identified and described by Sacks as the 'story' (1992,b:3-31). As has been suggested, from the point of view of conversation analysis, stories are an integral part of the manner through which topics (and therefore categories in talk) in conversation are sequentially managed (Coulthard 1975, Jefferson 1978, Goodwin 1981, Lynch and Bogen 1996 and Psathas 1996). For Sacks, a story may be relatively brief or longwinded. Sacks (April 9, 16th 1970) states:

> Since they take more than one utterance to produce, it is relevant that the recipient learns (hears) that a story is to be produced. Otherwise, because of the turn taking system of conversation, a speaker at a turn completion point may find that another person begins to speak. How it is that another person knows that it is not a place to speak since any next possible completion point is a place to speak. One way would be to produce an utterance which says that what I plan to say will take more than one

utterance and the number of utterances cannot be specified in advance. If this is accepted by the others, then the speaker may retain the right to speak over a series of utterances.

For Sacks stories are problematic, in terms of the speech exchange systems for conversation, in that speakers are likely to 'self select' in opening a story. They are designed for listeners without necessarily conforming to rules of relevance and the contingencies of previous utterances. Sacks also notes how stories are organised into story *prefaces*, the story *proper* and story *closings*. For Schenkein (1978:219), the story preface can be heard as a request to take an extended turn. The story preface, Schenkein argues, makes recognisable that something interesting or important is to follow. As Schenkein (1978:219) argues a request for an extended turn-in-talk is characterised by a:

> ... story preface in which a teller projects a forthcoming story, a next turn in which a co-participant aligns himself as a story recipient, a next in which a teller produces the story (a series of segments in which teller's talk can alternate with recipient's) and a next in which the story recipient talks by reference to the story. Further, the story preface can have consequences for the story's reception, and thus a rather extended series of turns at talk can be seen as a coherent conversational unit.

The story proper consists of a designed collection of categories, which are chosen or displayed in order to facilitate and realise the design potential of the story, such designs may resemble Sacks' (1992a: 299) description of 'request formats'. Request formats may consist of a story in which the categories displayed within the *story proper* facilitate and 'point to' the information that the 'story teller' wants to be heard. Such a method exhibits Sacks' observation that stories are primarily designed, as a conversational format, for the listener. However, stories have to be newsworthy, and concern themselves about something in particular.

A further dimension to the conceptualisation of the story presented in this chapter is the notion of accounts. In one sense all utterances are 'accountable' (Garfinkel 1967) in the sense that they reflexively constitute and display the sense of social organisation that is being locally accomplished by members on an ongoing 'no time out' basis. However, accounts can also be understood to refer to forms of talk that provide descriptions, explanations or justifications of activities, people, events and so forth. An account is not necessarily synonymous with a story. However, stories can often be understood to account, in terms of description, explanation and justification for various matters or events. This process of 'accounting' is tied to the topical content of story type utterances and can therefore be understood to be primarily organised in terms of categories.

To this extent, whilst stories can be viewed as sequential components within talk, they are also a means of *category display* (in the sense that the topical dimensions of a story are primarily categorial in nature). In terms of Sacks' work, we may argue that stories, as a means of having something to say, are also topically organised and therefore in terms of categorisation have to be coherent (Coulthard 1975). Furthermore, whilst coherence may be a design feature of an interlocutor's utterance, the sequential and categorial activity of recipient design (in the case of stories the design is primarily, although not in every case, for listeners and not previous speakers) provides a method through which 'coherence' is constituted as a displayable and recognisable feature of utterances. Thus we may, in the course of discussing stories and accounts, emphasise the intertwining, 'folding back' matrix of categorial and sequential methods (Watson 1997: 49-75). However, this is not a rigid or a formalistic distinction but a reflexive and mutually constitutive plane of local, in situ, reflexive, practical work of members accomplishing situated contingencies of social organisation and order. Thus, stories are both sequentially and categorially organised.

Stories as Normative Assessments, Descriptions and Accounts of Reality

A further dimension of the occasioned and locally produced character of stories in members' talk is the work that they do. This work is not necessarily tied to mentalistic conceptualisations of intention or personal goals but is an emergent property of the mutually constitutive character of members interaction. Lynch and Bogen (1996:280) note how note how certain moral entitlements are routineley accorded to story tellers. These entitlements can be understood to be categorially organised and consist of a normative and moral set of inferences that are derived from the story and accorded to the teller. These may consist of the teller having lived through an experience or having a unique or privileged access to an event or occurrence. Furthermore, these moral entitlements are also routinely tied to the various occasioned activities that the production of stories may occur within. For example, stories may be used as vehicles to recount experiences central to a criminal investigation or cross examination. They may also be elicited and deployed by members during activities within which matters relating to the truth and actual events are crucial (as in the Iran Contra Hearings elegantly analysed and explored by Lynch and Bogen). However, it must be emphasised that such activities are accomplished in and through the sequential and categorial organisation of talk and the moral-inferential apparatus of culture-in-action accomplished and displayed in and through members' talk. As Lynch and Bogen (1996:278) state:

> Numerous conversation-analytic studies have examined stories in conversation and their constituent structures... In the present study we focus more on issues of narrative design, moral entitlement, and the social distribution of stories; these are themes that also were central to Sacks's work on stories, but they have been given less attention within conversation analysis... The storyteller's presence in the story goes well beyond specific mentions of ego and of subjective meaning. For example, the selection of predicates to describe and juxtapose scenic details, the temporal ordering and sequencing of narrative phases, and the grammatical tense of the story all serve to establish the teller's place within events and to provide grounds for inferences regarding what happened and what its significance might be. Story tellers commonly deploy spatial and temporal predicates that are relative to the teller's and audience's past and present relations to the events in the story.

Stories can therefore be understood to be deployed in a variety of settings during the course of a number of activities. However, stories have been routinely shown to be part of a methodological apparatus deployed by members (in and through category and sequence in talk) that accounts for events through various discursive modalities (e.g. moral assessment, description or the sequential placement of an extended turn) and is often oriented towards the interactional accomplishment of specific forms of moral inference. Furthermore, as has been stated, this is also realised through the specific cultural entitlements accorded to story tellers.

In order to appreciate the occasioned relationship between category, sequence, moral inference and task displayed through stories within talk-in-interaction in more detail a consideration of the methodological approach to analysing stories in team talk-in-interaction adopted in this chapter will be provided. I will then seek to explicate these ideas through an analysis of story telling as it occurs within situated instances of team talk.

Analysis

The use of stories as a means of holding the floor, can be heard as a method of responding to difficult questions. Stories may be heard to provide prefaces which indicate (make recognisable) that an extended sequence is being taken up. The following extract involves an exchange of views, by team members, that concerns the problem of re-organising office space and the relocation of team members. The conversation followed the need to reorganise office space. This was due to the fact that certain members of the team were leaving the team to work elsewhere and relationships of some team members had developed and changed in accordance with work and employment that they were undertaking with different agencies and organisations.

Example One – Story Formats and Responses to Difficult Questions

```
1. CDW:No I'm sorry (0.5) well (1.0) there's **** there is *** there is **
2.        there's me and their's everybody in there and I can't operate I was going
3.        to raise the question earlier (0.5) but now I understand what your saying
4.        about (0.5) [your room ]
5.LVC:                [ How will ] you then operate if you stay there and come
6.        to the Community room are you going to tell these people to stay? =
7.CDW: = No No No they come and go that's my problem
8.C:     mmmm (.)
9.LVC:  So what's the difference between members of staff and members of the
10.       Community coming in?    [ doing ]
11.CDW:                           [ Wh:: ] (.) what's that (.) got to do with it
12.LVC: (intake of breath) doing what you have just complained about (.)
13.CDW:I'm not complaining about anything I actually agree that our room
14.       should be the smaller (0.5) but it hasn't worked out that's what I'm
15.       saying (0.5) I argued I voted for it (0.5) but it hasn't worked out so I'm
16.       now saying I'm agreeing though (name of SW3) is saying her room
17.       will be noisy cos we 're up there it won't (0.4) nothing compared to
18.       what it is in there at the moment (0.5) nothing (0.5) you can't get in
19.       there at times with people blowing and puffing and fucking Argos
20.       catalogues all over the gaff (1.5) So it has got to stop I can't work like
21.       that I'm sorry I can shout at you all day long but there is too many people
22.       (0.5) So I'm only suggesting that somebody has got to move around (0.5)
23.       a bit that's all.
```

The preceding extract can be heard to involve talk about a topic. The topic in question involves the reorganisation of office space and personnel. The CDW initiates a sequence that expresses a problem, the problem being that there are too many people who have access to his office. The LVC (L.5) responds to the CDW's utterance by asking that if the CDW changes offices (in this case the community room) will the remaining members of staff have to 'stay'? The end of the question is incomplete due to an interruption by the CDW who informs the last speaker that team members can come and go to the community room as they wish. The CDW states that it is his 'problem'. The LVC responds to this answer to the question by supplying a supplementary question. The LVC utilises the contrast class 'members of staff' and 'members of the community', as a means of questioning the validity of the CDW's claim (L.9, 10). In this case, there being to many people being around for him to work. The CDW responds by querying the relevance of the LVC's utterance.(L.11) The LVC replies to this query by referring to preface of the CDW's story,(L.12) namely the need to change rooms due to it being virtually impossible to operate due to the number of people having access to his work environment. In doing so, the LVC invokes the contrast class described above through the tying of community room with members of the community having access to the device 'community room'. This would presumably, the LVC infers, involve coming and going and therefore become a potential source of some of the problems the CDW initially complained about but tied to the membership categories of team members. This sequence involves a display of a category analysis by the LVC on the problem talk and story being told by the CDW. The LVC questions the logic of the CDW's reasons (which is a category analysis of sorts) by questioning the implicit distinction between the problems the CDW talks about and his belief that moving to the community room would 'solve' the problem. The LVC's questioning results in an extended turn (L.13-22).

The extended sequence that follows may be understood as a rebuttal of a 'difficult question'. In general terms, it involves a rejection of the LVC's analysis of the CDW's reasons for moving rooms. The CDW begins the account by stating 'I'm not complaining'. The CDW states that he agreed that his room should be 'smaller', but that it hadn't worked out. Furthermore, he adds that he 'voted' for the previous agreement. In some respects, this talk prefaces a 'rebuttal story'. He provides a history of his position in terms of the present arrangement. He then moves to the proposed problem that the LVC is attempting to identify. However, he doesn't explicitly refer to the distinction between staff and members of the community that the LVC identifies. Rather, he sticks to talk of 'rooms' that can be understood to form part of the device 'present office arrangements'. However, whilst he suggests that the proposed room may well be noisy it won't be as noisy as his present location. Consequently, the problem identified by the CDW is transposed to the predicate of 'noisiness' of which different proposed levels are ascribed to the locations in question. It is in this way that the CDW attempts to rebut the LVC's use of the contrast class, 'members of staff' and 'members of community' in questioning the CDW's previous position. However, the CDW continues by elaborating on the present condition of his room and thus, we are provided with a number of descriptions that refer to people smoking, shouting, bawling and teapots and catalogues being left all over the office. The CDW reasserts his previous pitch, namely, that there are too many people in his office and that he has been complaining about a need for change for quite some time. He concludes by stating 'somebody has got to move around a bit that's all'. The length of the sequence can be heard as a means of rebutting a difficult question. The CDW attempts to utilise noisiness as a means of dismissing the possibility, suggested by the LVC, that a move to the community room would not ameliorate the conditions of work that the CDW describes. Thus, the LVC's questioning is only answered via reference to different levels of noise. In one sense therefore, both the LVC and the CDW are attempting to secure different moral inferences for the device 'office working environment'. However, the predicate of noise was not initially referred to. The extended sequence can be heard to represent a means of downgrading the LVC's question. In terms of the local interactional economy, an extended sequence may be heard as an attempt to answer a difficult question by embellishing claims already made. The reference to potentially differing levels of noise in the community room is the only recognisable response to the LVC's question. Furthermore, the distinction\contrast class that the LVC establishes is not referred to. It is not oriented to as a topic or recognised as a useful analysis of the problem. The embellishment surrounding the singular attempt to deal with the LVC's question may indicate an attempt to gloss over the point through the use of a story format.

The following extract involves talk recorded at an Allocation meeting. It involves a discussion concerning problems and clients that the team is in contact with. In particular, the discussion is concerned with elderly clients who have serious medical conditions and the support that the overstreched social service agencies can provide. Furthermore, the discussion begins through an account of an individual working with such clients who, we are told, is feeling bad about the predicament of elderly clients and the difficulties in meeting the needs of such vulnerable people.

Example Two – Short Stories and Client Description

1.TL: I saw (Y) on Thursday (1.0) she was saying she feels very guilty because
2.   (1.0) bec (0.5) well she feels like (0.5) (she's ?) leaving them in a
3.   dumping ground
4.All: mmm =
5.TL: =So I told her not to worry because it's a bit of problem (1.0) obviously
6.   the ones were going to get are going to be serious which errr (4.0)
7.SW3: When I applied for a phone for the (name of clients) (.)
8.All: mmm (.)
9.SW3: Yeah (1.0) this woman was (1.0) at the time she was very (0.5) terminally
10.   ill (0.5) she was walking about and is still (1.5) inoperable (1.0) you
11.   know what I mean? (5.0)

12.TL: Anybody have anything else they wish to share? (.)
13.SW1:Yeah (0.5) my child care orders (1.0) are quite interesting. John's not
14.   going to be the problem it's the parents (1.0) both of them (1.0) it's like
15.   parents rule over anxious (0.5) real tense lot (0.5) real tense lot (0.4)
16.   tackling it all th' (1.5) next day(.)
17.All: mm   [m mmm]
18.(?)   [Yeah   ].

In the extract above, we are met with a number of utterances that consist of a condensed version of the story format. That is to say whilst the talk does not consist of a long extended turn the talk is characterised by sequences that are relatively long in duration. The turn taking in this stretch of talk is not symmetrical but characterised by a certain degree of asymmetry between contextually short utterances (e.g. questions L.6,11 and prompts L.3,7,16 and affirmations L.17) and contextually long utterances that can be understood as a condensed form of the story format (L.1-5, 8-10 and 12 - 15). These utterances can be understood as a condensed form of the story format in the sense that they are prefaced, consist of a story 'proper' (in this case a specific message) and are, apart from the first example in this extract, closed effectively. Furthermore, they are forms of utterance that are initiated and requested by the Team Leader. The floor becomes open for condensed story formats that account for particular descriptions of clients and cases that the Team are dealing with. Thus, like longer story formats observed during the course of team talk and interaction, they are oriented towards accounting for events and business associated with the flood support team's work.

The first involves the initiation of a topic namely the account provided by the team leader that refers to the experience of an external worker who 'feels very guilty' about leaving certain clients 'in a dumping ground'. The clients referred to in this extract are elderly people who are terminally ill, a point referred to in this extract but established in talk before this particular stretch of conversation. The first part of the condensed story namely, the introduction of an external worker (Y) who has reported these experiences, is met by a set of prompts by team members (i.e. the 'mmmm' insertion at L.3). The team leader continues by reporting his response to the external worker's dilemma, namely that it is a bit of a 'problem' (L.4). The team leader attempts to close his account through reference to the 'ones' (namely elderly terminally ill people) which may be referred to the team. The display of 'errr' can be *recognised* as an inability to select a suitable category or predicate to which his closing utterance is designed to include (L.5). In other words, the team leader displays and makes recognisable an inability to describe the type of 'terminally ill elderly people' that the team may have had referred to them. This elicitation is met by a four-second pause, there is no immediate self-selection. In one sense, the inability to describe the type of terminally elderly people that the team may have under its care suggests that there are no criteria or associated set of available predicates of the 'flood support team' that can be tied to 'terminally ill elderly people', 'them' or 'the ones' as the category of client group is variously described within the talk. The problem of terminally ill elderly people in the community stands outside the parameters of 'flood support'. Within the rubric of flood support, other 'problems' within the community cannot be tied to the device of 'the flood' easily. Other devices or descriptions which may have been chosen include social problems, lack of health care for elderly people and poverty. These cannot be selected via the use of 'we', the pro-term standing on behalf of 'the Flood Support Team'. Thus, we may infer that flood support (as a set of activities) cannot be easily, in terms of practical reasoning, be reconciled to the support, treatment and care of terminally ill, elderly people unless they are also explicitly categorised as flood victims.

Following the pause, SW3 self selects and refers to an experience by providing a preface to her condensed story (L.6) that involves applying for a phone for one of her clients. The preface is acknowledged through the display of 'continuers', namely the cacophony of 'mmm's (L.7). SW3 begins an account which corresponds to a second story format, in that it leads on, in terms of recipient design and topic, from the team leader's first story. We are informed of a woman who was 'very ill', 'walking about' and was 'inoperable'. Here, we note how the story structure is sequentially and categorially organised. We are then introduced to a description of the woman that can be heard to belong to a number of membership categories and devices. For example, we may hear it as a category of 'flood victim' or 'client'. However, in terms of recipient design and the secondary story format we hear it as belonging to the category of 'elderly terminally ill people'.[1] The predicates that follow affirm this reading in that they are associations, attributes and activities tied to the aforementioned device (L.9). SW3 then closes with a question, 'do you know what I mean?' this is followed by a pause for about five seconds. No one immediately selects himself or herself to speak, the problem of describing terminally ill people remains conversationally recognisable but it has become an unsafe topic.

This pause is then followed by the team leader self-selecting a turn (L.11) that, in fact, is merely a further invitation for other team members to have a turn. The team members are invited to produce a similar type of sequence (i.e. a condensed story type account). This is achieved through the elicitation of the request, 'anybody else have anything they wish to share?' (L.10). Clearly, this may involve an invitation to change topic but also to 'share' something. This something is a story similar to those that have been elicited beforehand, and can be understood as a conversational concession for inviting a change from the unsafe (and praxiologically and categorially problematic) topic of terminally ill people. Consequently, sharing is not an explicit request to recipient categorial design as such, but an invitation to talk about a 'newsworthy topic' in terms of the condensed format displayed in this stretch of team talk. In this sense, sharing is not only the provision of a 'newsworthy item' but also the display of symmetry in the sequential organisation of the next utterance.

The next utterance is sequentially symmetrical and 'newsworthy'. However, the topic has changed a precondition of taking this particular turn. It begins with a preface, that includes references to 'child care orders' (L.12) and categories of person (of the device flood victim). The categories of person consist of references to the client's name and his parents. Through the use of the clients name and reference to 'parents' we understand that the client and case is not only tied to the device of 'flood victim' or 'social work client', but also to the device of the 'family'. The problem here is that the parents are 'anxious' and a 'real tense lot' and that such associations and attributes are representative of 'parents rule' (L.13, 14). The parents are therefore described in terms of predicated attributes which may also be tied to the device 'states of mind' or individual psychology. This claim is not explicitly made, but the predication, in terms of the weak form of recognisability[2] makes such a reading available in terms of the member oriented features of problem talk and story telling.

In this instance the condensed stories are designed to display information about clients. However, such information is mediated by the activity of sharing stories and responding to cases that do not fit easily with the task of flood support. This is illustrated by the first story that refers to problem cases of elderly terminally ill people being handled by members of a different team. Consequently, we can hear how stories are being used as a means of paying attention to the topic of problematic cases. Furthermore, the presentation of the case story after the team leaders invitation can be heard as the type of problem case that does fit into the domain of flood support. Thus, in this case stories are being used to recognisably demarcate what constitutes flood support and what does not. The use of condensed story formats may indicate that the team members have little time to address team issues at this particular meeting. On the other hand it may also be related to the topic of sharing information about clients in allocation meetings within a team that is unfamiliar with this form of activity.

During the course of the final extract the team are discussing the future of funding for the team and the important relationship that such matters have with local *councillors* (i.e. holders of local political office who have an effect on decisions concerning social service budgets and funding for the specific team in question). The team leader and the counsellor are relating a story about their experiences of a trip to a community function at which some members of the local council were present. The story is being related to the topic about the future funding of the team's work.

Example Three – The Story as a Co-jointly Produced Ethno-epistemological Device

1.TL: Well there were alot of councillors there but none (.) few of them came
2.   around
3.C: Didn't come near us (.) (name of a councillor) did (.) what was the
4.   councillor who spoke to us oh (.) the lady (.) the woman (.) she was
5.   Queen Victoria last year (.)
6. TL: = Oh yes =
7. C: = In the Victorian extravaganza I know her name (.) y'know she was (.)
8.   SAYING everybody's fine *now* I know *a lot* of *people* and they were *all*
9.   *fine* (.) they're all *coping* (.) they were the *only* two (.)
10.LVC: We need to get in touch with the council and start kicking butts (.)
11.SW1: No, No
12.LVC: Tell em straight =
13.C: = People like (name of councillor) and th::at (.)
14.LVC: If the council begin to think that (.) if the council reckon that then we are
15.   finished(.)
16.All: ermm
17.TL: Yeah (.)
18.C: I think the councillors some of them (.) who knows (.) so and so knows
19.   me I've worked for him (.) they were keeping away.

During the course of this extract the team leader and the counsellor co-jointly produce a story. The opening of the account is produced (L.1-3) and related to a community function at which some local councillors were present. We are told that there were a number of them (L.1) and that most of them did not come near, and therefore presumably speak, to the team members present (L.2). The counsellor then produces a description about one of the councillors who had dressed up as Queen Victoria at a carnival event the preceding year. The significance of this piece of information is that the carnival was a Victorian extravaganza and therefore dressing up as Queen Victoria denotes a degree of importance. This description of one of the councillors is supported by an affirmation by the team leader (L.4). The preface of the story is then completed.

The counsellor continues by providing the story proper, namely what this particular (important) councillor said about the flood which the team are dealing with. We are told that she referred to people she knew in the flood hit community as being 'fine' and 'okay' (L.6). The story is closed by reference to the fact that the lady councillor in question was one of only two councillors who spoke to them. As the account is closed the LVC (L.8) displays an assessment of the story that has just been produced. He states that the council needs to be contacted and lobbied vigorously. This assessment displays an understanding of the stories situated logic, namely the fact that not many of the councillors who were present talked to the team members during the event and the one councillor who did considered the worst to be over. This represents an underlying documentary inference in the sense that the council, as a whole, no longer considers flood support to be priority and therefore funding for the team (and people who are still in need) is in jeopardy.

The LVC's assessment and call for action is met by disagreement by SW1 (L.9). The LVC elaborates on his assessment by stating that the team should 'tell them straight' (L.10). The counsellor responds to this further utterance by identifying which people might be targeted, namely the councillor featured in the story. The LVC then develops his assessment by stating that if the 'council think like that' then 'we are finished' (L.12). This story is being used as a resource to infer the council's view of the flood and the flood support team in terms of continued funding. This assessment is met by affirmation by the team members' (L.13). The close of this extract involves a 'skip connection' by the counsellor back to the initial story. She adds a further piece to the story, namely that some of the councillors knew her and were deliberately keeping away (L.16).

In this extract we can see how the co-produced story is used as a resource by the team to search for underlying patterns as a means of addressing the topic of funding and flood support. The underlying pattern that the story presents to the team members can be understood to be located in the reported opinion that one of the councillors conveyed to the counsellor at the community function. However, an additional underlying pattern is also being used as a resource to make inferences about the councils intentions for the team. This is contained within the story but is made overtly recognisable by the counsellors' skip connection (L.16) that refers to the fact that most of the councillors at the community function kept away from the team leader and counsellor. In this sense, proximity is being used as a resource for methodically drawing up a picture of the council's intentions. The LVC's reference to the council thinking in a particular manner is realised through the way in which councillors (as membership categories) are part of the collection i.e. device of the council. Furthermore, through the invocation of the hearers maxim, the categorisation of one member of the population as viewing the effects of the flood as over (in the sense that most flood victims were now fine) provides for an adequate description for all members of that population.

Consequently, the device of the council thinking in a particular way is established.

In this extract we can see how stories can be co-jointly produced and used as a resource for informing topical discussion and assessing organisational matters. Stories are both sequentially and categorially organised. In this case the story provides a resource for establishing the councils motives and intentions. The story is therefore an epistemological device, in this instance, which provides information, but also draws upon members methods (as a feature of its design) in assessing the reality of a specific situation i.e. team funding and flood support.

Conclusion

During this application of sequential and categorial analysis of the transcribed data a number of points may be put forward. The examination of meetings has often ignored the local conversational machinery of meetings as situated accomplishments of an ongoingly achieved and interactionally constituted order. The spectre of external considerations has been expressed in terms of specified grammars for interaction within meetings. The description of the meeting as a resource for teamwork has taken notions such as dialogue, understanding, meaning and the exchange of information for granted. The examination of the local conversational machinery of meetings provides for a respecification of such theorised descriptions by illustrating the way in which members utilise specific methods in attempting to deal with the emergent contingencies of doing the order of a meeting. Indeed, by locating such emergent properties within the context of members' praxiological work the possibility of investigating processes that are fundamental to teamwork can be realised. Much of the literature (e.g. Øvretveit 1994) dealing with teamwork does not examine those processes but assume they are present. The precise details of how such generalised descriptions tally with the lived work of doing team meetings remains unspecified, poorly documented and misunderstood.

The activity of topic management and the elicitation of extended sequences in the form of stories can therefore be understood to be part and parcel of the methods through which the local organisation of a team meeting is accomplished, how information is exchanged and opinions expressed. To this extent stories are embedded and situated within the task of carrying out the activity of the team and allocation meetings. Furthermore, through the analysis of stories as embedded phenomena, the variety of functions and uses that such formats can be put to can be more fully appreciated. To this extent the story as a simple mechanism of disclosure has to be rejected in favour of a model that provides for the multi-dimensional character of stories and story telling in members's talk in work-organisational settings. Furthermore, the application of the reconsidered model of membership categorisation analysis to the task of addressing the situated character of members talk provides for a means of more fully documenting and describing the manner through which narrative talk is occasioned and produced as a means of pursuing member-relevant activities.

An additional consideration at this stage of the chapter is the moral character of stories that seek to account for events, clients and experiences. As the Lynch and Bogen quote, referred to earlier in this chapter, makes clear stories are part of the apparatus of moral inference. Furthermore, as Sacks (1992 a, b) has illustrated so elegantly and convincingly culture has to be respecified as an inferential machine that is an ongoing process manifested in members actions rather than a scenic backdrop within which social action is made sense from in much the same way as a set painted figures in a C19th century painting of a pastoral setting. Indeed, the political content and character of stories as *situated* accounting mechanisms is perhaps easier to grasp for those sociologists who do not privilege the political sphere with quite the same objective grace and sense of ontological permeation into the 'social' as certain macro-model conceptualisations of economy or culture. Provided one can accept the notion of culture-in-action, it is clear that the analysis of stories and so forth may aid the analysis of role as an interactional device and resource (Housley 1999) within organisational contexts.

In conclusion, the demarcation of story sequences into structure and function glosses over the manner through which function and structure are locally occasioned and reflexively constituted phenomena that are mutually elaborative (i.e. each informs the other). Stories and narrative sequences, in members' talk, are designed and constructed in situations that may invite overlap, interruption, questioning and disagreement. The multifaceted dimensions and situated social organisation of story telling stand in contrast to the generation of functional taxonomies of narrative in members' talk. Whilst the designation of formal properties in talk and the application of general properties (e.g. occupational socialisation) to particular cases may aid theoretical construction they detract from the in situ character of members talk (which may, in this case, be of particular interest to practitioners and people working within social/care work teams). To this extent whilst stories in talk-in-interaction can be understood to have a number of identifiable properties these properties may be constituted and displayed in a number of different ways within different conversational activities and contexts. Thus, stories may come in a number of different 'extended formats' relative to the site and context of their production. Furthermore, they may be produced by more than one speaker and, as has been stated, be subject to overlap, interruption and so forth. To this extent the character of communication within team based settings and the associated predicates of exchanging information and so forth can be heard to be of a more complex and detailed nature than model oriented accounts suggest.

Notes

1   That is to say that this description is duplicatively organised in that it is part of the collection, 'population' but is then becomes a device\collection in terms of SW1's use of the term woman and the modes of predication that follow.

2   As has been argued a further feature of Sacks' explication of conversational interaction is 'recognisability'. For Sacks, the identifiable features of talk are necessarily recognisable to members-in-talk. In short, the process of making certain conversational work recognisable, provides for the orienting features of talk, they provide the basis of the interactional and social premise through which conversational interaction is possible. Thus, the comprehension of a joke is dependent not only on the conversational methods employed, but also that the recognisability of the turn-taking system, and the conventions of the 'joke' as a technical, methodically achieved object, being recognised by the recipients of the proffered joke. Indeed, as Watson (1997) notes, recognisability, in the form of recipient design, is a way in which members routinley display this principle in terms of the design features of their utterances.

7 Team Members' Perceptions and Theorising Team Structures

One of the important topics that this investigation into multidisciplinary teams generates is the issue of theorising team structures. Clearly the work carried out on teams in recent years is thorough, considered and worthy of the greatest consideration. However, it is my contention that models of multidisciplinary team work and so forth would benefit from a consideration of research into how roles, knowledge, expertise and communication actually operate *in situ.* In other words, from the perspective and research observations being advanced here model generation should utilise real wordly data in designing ideal types and templates for policy implementation. The ways in which team members make sense, interact and so forth should form the pragmatic basis though which team design and organisation be built around. The explanatory power of functionalist theorising is not matched by real wordly specifics. The discoverable formal properties of practical reasoning do not sit well with such an edifice. Indeed, a consideration of the ways in which members attempt to accomplish the activities of team work and multidisciplinarity is a valuable resource for evidenced based policy and practice.

During the course of this book I have sought to examine a number of aspects of the situated praxiological work of a multidisciplinary team. From an ethnomethodological position I am unable to provide a set of findings or conclusions which can be read to be representative or valid in terms of some objective, neo–positivistic schema. However, this investigation has examined and described, in detail, the situated dimension of the work of a multidisciplinary team. My interest has been to account for a range of singular activities that the analysis of the data has yielded. Whilst a range of objections may be raised against such an approach it is nonetheless one which is rigorous and grounded within a solid corpus of observational studies. Michael Lynch and David Bogen (1997) note how the activities of thick description and the analysis of situated singular activities have been criticised. However, drawing from the Wittgenstein (and the ethnomethodological tradition) they note how the great

116

philosopher promoted the activity of describing singular (situated) activities over and above the craving for generality that had led to so many theoretical 'cul de sacs'. Lynch and Bogen (1997:270) state:

> Wittgenstein's renunciation of the craving for generality in favour of description may seem quaint in light of the prevailing tendencies to consider "pure description" as an epistemological impossibility, and it may recall the sorts of avowals of neutral, value-free description so often criticised these days for disguising an author's normative slant and deleting the contingencies involved in the construction of such descriptions. Again, it may be seem that from Wittgenstein we have adopted an unsophisticated conception of discourse that has been surpassed by more recent developments in literary and cultural studies...Wittgenstein is not endowing description with a special epistemological status; indeed, he is arguing against the craving for generality, which he described as a "contemptuous attitude towards the particular case." Such a contemptuous attitude denigrates mere description for its failure to subordinate the concrete details of a case to a theoretically specified foundation, ideology, or generalised discourse. For Wittgenstein, descriptions of singular activities are valuable precisely because they cast into relief diverse, unexpected, yet intelligible organisations of language use.

Consequently, this book must be considered in terms of the above. Within this chapter I will seek to reflect on the analyses carried out during previous chapters and provide a summary of my observations and descriptions of situated aspects of singular interactional activities within the multidisciplinary team context(s) explored. I will also seek to reflect upon other aspects of this study, namely the accounts of multidisciplinarity discussed in chapter one and the process of researching social care contexts utilising an ethnomethodological approach.

A Summary of Observations and Descriptions of Singular Situated Instances of Team Members' Talk within Multidisciplinary Team Meetings

The following observations provide a summary of the analysis of team members situated interactional work within the multidisciplinary team contexts examined. Consequently, they must be read as the summary of a thick description of the situated and singular activities of team members *in situ.*

Exchanging Information, Dialogue and Discussion within Team Meetings

In terms of the interactional instances examined, the principles of exchanging information, dialogue and discussion can be respecified in terms of a complex and detailed array of conversational methods and organisation. The studies within this book illustrate how such work is methodically accomplished. In contrast to this, the models of multidisciplinarity outlined during the initial stages of this book fail to take account of the praxiological, in situ and interactionally achieved context that such a proposed set of communicative processes attempt to encapsulate. These general descriptions 'take for granted' the conversational and interactional competencies of members in a way which does not seem to be considered within the models of multidisciplinary working evident in some of Øvretveit's (1993) recommendations.

The way in which members carry out conversational work within team meetings can be seen to consist of a series of haeccetic achievements that are accomplished in situ. Consequently, notions such as 'the exchange of information' should consider the praxiological, reflexive, mutually constitutive and conversational methods of such work. Furthermore, the principle methods of such interactional activity can be understood in terms of the local management of categories-in-talk. This involves sequential organisation of talk and modes of category display that can be understood to be mutually elaborative. In many respects, the exchange of information, dialogue and communication can be understood as foundational precepts within the general models and other theoretical descriptions of multidisciplinarity discussed in the beginning of this book. As such, the studies presented here can be seen to respecify such models in terms of members in vivo methods which have been observed, outlined, discussed and analysed with respect to the local specificity of naturally occurring conversational interaction within a number of multidisciplinary team meetings and settings.

Role and Team Structure within Multidisciplinary Teams

The notion of role and 'team structure' evident in the theoretical postulations and recommendations for multidisciplinary team practice is one which is essentially structural functionalist in character (e.g. Øvretveit 1996). Roles are seen to slot into different types of team structure in a systems type configuration. The studies within this book have sought to illustrate how 'role' is an interactionally achieved resource that is reflexively monitored, strategically deployed and praxiologically realised. Roles can be observed to be interactionally achieved materials which members may invoke as a means of carrying out various activities associated with doing a team meeting. For example, the downgrading and upgrading of accounts or the ethno-epistemological work of validating ones claims have been observed and understood to utilise the conversationally achieved device/resource of 'role' as a means of achieving such practical objectives. The presentation of 'role' as a monolithic script which provide the contours for interactional activity within multidisciplinary meetings disregards the occasioned and locally produced features of role both as an interactional device and situated accomplishment. In terms of 'team structure' the Team can be heard to be an interactional accomplishment that is praxiologically and methodically achieved, rather than a contextual backdrop to which members mystically slot into or simply find a role within. The Team can therefore be understood as a locally produced form of social organisation that is interactionally sustained and reproduced.

Knowledge, 'Know-how' and Multidisciplinary Meetings

As chapter five illustrated the interactional achievement of 'know-how' can be respecified as a situational accomplishment within which members deploy a range of methods in making claims, upgrading/downgrading accounts and accomplishing relevance through the sequential and categorical organisation of talk. One of the most striking features of these accounts is the way in which recognisability, through the sequential structure of adjacency pairs and recipient design within the meetings examined, produces accounts which are mutually elaborative, locally produced and realised within the contextual conversational specifics of the talk-in-meetings. As has been stated, the notion of identifiable and clearly observable 'knowledge bases' which are representative of disciplines being consistently displayed by relevant team members (e.g. the counsellor and psychotherapeutic discourse) have not been observed within this case study.

Through the methodical work of constituting role distinctions and recognising knowledge or expertise in talk, multidisciplinarity can be understood to be located firmly in members' interactional work rather than through the structures discussed in textual accounts of multidisciplinarity. This is not to deny that such configurations are not useful, merely that the lived orderliness of multidisciplinary teamwork is not captured or considered by such forms of discourse. However, in the case of *this (and only this) study* the notion of identifiable and clearly observable 'knowledge bases' being displayed by relevant team members was not observed. The interactional mileux of the team and the character of making sense to one and each other may mean that such a practical strategy of clearly observable displays of knowledge is on that does not make practical sense. Consequently, the display of 'different view points' generated from different disciplinary or professional perspectives may take on a more camouflaged, or implicit, guise.

Epistemology and Multidisciplinarity

Multidisciplinarity is an epistemological enterprise insofar as it aims to provide a more holistic account of reality and truth by utilising a number of different knowledge bases as a means of realising this objective. The assumption being that a variety of approaches provide for a fuller, more whole and therefore 'better' connection with reality. In terms of multidisciplinarity and the meetings examined, epistemology is also a consideration for members. The process of making claims, upgrading accounts and downgrading other accounts often involves the use of ethno-epistemological strategies for validating utterances. These conversational methods for connecting members' accounts with the 'truth' or 'reality' do not conform to the natural scientific method (i.e. hypothesis, observation and deduction) or the principles of logic. Rather, they appeal to modes of justification grounded in terms of 'what we all know', that is to say assemblages of commonsense knowledge and the praxiological register which are available, accountable and recognisable features of team members talk. These methods for making sense stand outside the prescriptive formula of policy recommendations and hypothesised accounts. The manner through which events are accounted for stands in contrast to theoretical accounts of decision making. An appreciation of these types of understandings and practical formula for doing the teams work are often hidden from view, however an illustration of these practices serves to reminds us of the practical character of sense making, agreement and understanding in teams.

Communicative Ethics and the Situated Character of Team Members' Talk

The examination of instances of talk within this book has illustrated the situated character of members' talk within multidisciplinary settings. The notion that the formal parameters of the team's work influences or informs talk, is one that my description of singular interactional activities has eschewed. Consequently, the notion that there is a conversational bedrock, a normative framework for talk that contrasts with formal or institutionalised discourse is not discernible in *this* study. Therefore, the normative framework that institutional talk implies is questioned. Furthermore, the notion that talk can be placed within a framework of recognisable discursive structures is eschewed in favour of an examination of the situated detail of local discourse. In terms of multidisciplinarity and team talk, it seems reasonable to assert that such a configuration is something that members negotiate within the situated specifics of their daily work. Furthermore, as Lynch and Bogen (1997) note, the possibility of linking institutional talks' notion of asymmetry (and the distinction between mundane talk and institutional talk) with a neo-Habermasian communicative ethics is tempting. As Lynch and Bogen (1997:285) argue:

> There are obvious attractions to an attempt to analyse and evaluate specific systems and occasions of discourse by reference to "naturally organised" system for establishing protoethical rights and obligations to speak and listen. Among these attractions is the possibility of reconciling ethnomethodology's micro researches with more general social-theoretical models and normative programs.

The possibility of attempting to tie the Institutional Talk Programmes (henceforth referred to as ITP) analysis of 'pragmatic norms' within institutional settings (and the related baseline assumption of mundane conversation as an unforced exchange of utterances) is viewed by Lynch and Bogen (1997:285) as having surface affinity with the notion of communicative ethics, ideal speech acts and distorted communication advanced by Habermas (1990). With respect to the Iran Contra Hearings and Oliver North's testimony Lynch and Bogen state that the formal machinery of interrogation could not be viewed simply in terms of domination, control or any other pre-specified normative characteristics (expressed through sequential asymmetrical patterns in talk). Rather, according to Lynch and Bogen (1997:286):

> ... in our view, the idea that interrogation is a method of domination assumes too determinate a picture of testimony. Guided by the startling empowerment, at the time, of North by the very interrogative machinery that one might have thought was weighted in favor of his interrogators on the joint House-Senate committees, we began to grasp how North and his allies did not simply seize hold of a pre-given system of discursive levers; they did not simply reverse the force of an interrogative machinery and turn it against its operators. Instead, the actions of North and his colleagues selectively, collusively and unobtrusively relativised the

operative speech-exchange system [s] in which, and through which, they acted.

An additional point here stems from the reconciliation between categories and sequence in talk. Having established the manner through which sequences can become relative, made to work within the situated specifics of the task at hand, then the means through which this is achieved can be seen to be bound up with categories in talk. Indeed, as indicated during chapter two, Watson (1997) has noted the mutual elaborative texture of sequence and categories in talk. Within chapter four, the notion of the local management of categories was used as a means of illustrating the way through which sequential methods were used to locally manage and organise category flow in team members' conversation within multidisciplinary meetings. Consequently, from this position, I would seek to suggest that the ethnomethodological analysis of team members' talk within multidisciplinary meetings cannot be seen to be tied to any pre-formulated structure of action (textual or otherwise). To this extent, within *this study*, the models of multidisciplinarity and teamwork outlined in chapter one, and reflected upon at the beginning of this chapter, do not provide a form of life or normative apparatus which team members slot into or enact. Furthermore, any attempt to provide an account of formal/institutionalised properties of multidisciplinary meetings would negate the *occasioned character of such talk*. As Lynch and Bogen (1997:287) assert:

> The key point for considering the relevance of conversation or any other determinate system of speech exchange (including the abstract construct "talk-in – interaction") is that see no reason to figure that *any single* context-free system should necessarily hold fast as a foundation, as abase system establishing rules, when we play our various language games.

Indeed, this can be observed in the situated specifics of how utterances within the language games described within multidisciplinary team meetings were recognised as knowledgeable or valid (chapter five). In other cases (chapter six) utterances were designed in such a way as to make claims in meetings, using conversational forms of justification, which were highly situated in character and could not be understood in terms of pre-specified schema or parameters of institutional action. Indeed a sense of institutionality can be understood to comprise of retrospective 'repair' work.

Thus, in the case of the ethnomethodological examination of a multidisciplinary team the pre-specified models of multidisciplinary teamwork similarly fail to capture the situated conversational activity of team members. Furthermore, even if a program had sought to specify some formal properties of talk within multidisciplinary meetings, I hope that my study of singular conversational interaction within multidisciplinary meetings might lead some to consider the situated specifics of members' talk. As opposed to generalising about diverse methods and activities of members engaged in the local production of a 'multidisciplinary team order'. Thus, the analyses carried out in this book is characteristic of the post-analytic ethnomethodological approach espoused by Lynch and Bogen (1997:287) who state:

> Our descriptions are assailable, defeasible accounts, uncommitted to any single analytical model of conversational pragmatics or communicative ethics. Our ethnomethodological approach therefore is postanalytical in the sense that we presume that, and selectively describe how, the sources of intelligible action and defensible judgement are not contained within even the most elaborate system of prescriptions and specifications.

Having explored and summarised some of the issues raised in this book as they relate to communication, rationality and the situated character of team members talk I will now consider how such a perspective may aid those practitioners, working similar fields, professional development.

Reflective Practice and Practitioner Based Research: Some Observations

Therefore, it is clear that this study cannot be viewed in terms that are attempting to generalise about multidisciplinarity and teamwork. However, as a collection of detailed descriptions of occasioned singularities of talk and interaction within multidisciplinary team meetings I hope it will be a useful resource (and hopefully, a topic of enquiry in it's own right) for people interested in the interactional dimension of multidisciplinary teamwork. In terms of recent developments, within practitioner based studies, it might also provide a way for carrying out and extending the concerns of reflective practice within professional work settings (Schön 1991). Indeed, in recent years reflective practice has been promoted and tied to the process of practitioner based research. Practitioner based research is an idea which promotes research into professional activity/work by professionals or practitioners themselves. Everitt et al (1992) argue that a reflexive, practitioner based research programme should be used as a means of reclaiming the professionalism of social care/work from managerialism and "bourgeois improvers" (1992:3). Fuller and Petch (1995) argue that a reflexive approach to practitioner based research should be promoted as a means of enhancing basic professional skills. These professional skills are identified as producing more informed ways of being accountable, increasing the standing of the profession and to ensure a research base that is sympathetic to social work values (1995:8). Fuller and Petch (1995:52) list a number of strategies for data collection namely, the analysis of secondary sources, monitoring devices, questionnaires, interviews, scales and schedules, observation and diaries. The *ways* in which such data is analysed is described in terms of coding structured and unstructured data in order to generate statistical findings (1995:81-86). Fuller and Petch also discuss the important issues surrounding practitioner based research and the difficulties of practitioners carrying out research in the work place.

As I have suggested elsewhere the analysis of members' communicative and interactive activities within meetings (and potentially other contexts) could provide a way through which practitioners could reflect upon and analyse aspects of their own practice (Housley and Fitzgerald, 2000). Clearly, the methodological issues and problems of negotiating access (Hammersley and Atkinson 1995:54), managing field relations within a practitioner based setting that you are a part of and setting up a study would still very much apply. Furthermore, the use of a reconsidered model of membership categorisation analysis (Housley and Fitzgerald, 2002) would, through the attention to the situated specifics of members work, provide for the reflexive means of considering the practices of practitioners and of exploring the fine interactional detail of practitioners work. Therefore, the task of improving professional skills and developing the research base of the profession would be served by the adoption of such an approach as part of the repertoire of practitioner based research. As a reflexive enterprise, the analysis of the interactional specifics, instances and detail of members communicative work could be a rich resource for the goal of 'thinking in action' (Schön 1991). As Schön (1991:139) argues with respect to the principle of 'thinking in action':

> Seeing *this* situation as *that* one, one may also *do* in this situation as in that one. When a beginning physics student sees a pendulum problem as a familiar inclined plane problem, he can set up the new problem and solve it, using procedures both similar to and different from those he has used before. Just as he sees the new problem as a variation on the old one, so his new problem-solving behaviour is a variation of the old.

The process of thinking in action can therefore be seen to be a process through which the situated specifics of members activities provides a resource through which further activities (which may be distinct and unique) can be negotiated and made sense of. This may be achieved by reflecting on past (unique) experiences that may possess certain matrices of familiarity that can be brought to bear on the task at hand. To this extent, ethnomethodological-based analyses may be of use in disrupting natural attitudinal expectations and perceptions and providing a means of i.) reflecting on practice through analysis and ii.) reflecting on pieces of disseminated research and study. Furthermore, Garfinkel's argument that members of a society are not cultural dopes can be seen to be relevant in the case of practitioner based research. From an ethnomethodological point of view, members' methods and members' work are not merely the primary foci of study but can also viewed as the means through which practical activities are achieved. Clearly members, in the sense that Coulon (1996) uses the term, refer to members of a given linguistic group or speech community that social work and other social care practitioners may be seen to constitute. Schön (1991:269) in his discussion of reflective practice within the professions argues that variations between professions can also be contrasted with specific constants. Schön (ibid) argues that these constants provide for a means of considering the variation of reflective practice between different professions. According to Schön (1991:270) these can be described in terms of the following:

- The media, languages, and repertoires that practitioners use to describe reality and conduct experiments
- The appreciative systems they bring to problem setting, to the evaluation of inquiry, and to reflective conversation
- The overarching theories by which they make sense of phenomena
- The role frames within which they set their tasks and through which they bound their institutional settings.

Schön (ibid) elaborates on this framework by stating:

In calling these thing constants, I do not mean to suggest that they are absolutely unchanging. They do change, sometimes in response to reflection, but at a slower rate than theories of particular phenomenon or frames for particular problematic situations. Hence they give the practitioner the relatively solid references from which, in reflection-in-action, he can allow his theories and frames to come apart.

The studies within this book cannot be described as practitioner based research. However, as indicated earlier, the studies and analyses may be of use to practitioners. Furthermore, during the course of undertaking this study and producing this book the process of analysis has made me reflective of my own practice in my own specific work setting (as a seminar tutor, lecturer and so forth). Consequently, whilst this cannot be held up to be an objective proposal I would suggest that the analysis of situated action (in classrooms, meetings etc) would be consistent with a program of reflective practitioner based research. Furthermore, this book *may* provide a framework for those practitioners who are interested in familiarising themselves with the analysis of talk-in-interaction and extending the approach into their work setting as a means of meeting some of the objectives outlined by Schön, Fuller and Petch. Furthermore, in terms of Schön's (1991:270) four 'constants' I would argue that the analytical chapters in this book reflect these constants in terms of the concerns of an *ethnomethodological* approach. The concern with the interactional accomplishment of role, the local management of categories within team members talk, knowledgeability and ethno - epistemology can be see to address these constants in terms of the interactional and situated specifics of team members talk.

Reflections

The following observations and remarks are not empirical claims, advice or recommendations. Rather, they are a collection of further reflections that have been generated from the situated analyses carried out during the course of the analyses and arguments covered during the course of this book. I do not seek to legitimate such claims by citing observations that I have made during the course of my analysis of the situated particulars of members' work within the team settings examined. However, some reflection on the ethnomethodological notion of respecification and the field of social policy will be provided.

Situated Studies in Social Policy

The respecification of the conceptual apparatus within social policy and social administration provides for a possibility to develop a concern with the way in which interactive orders are accomplished. It may be argued that social policy and social administration have noted such concerns through the ethnographic work of Goffman (1967) and other interactionist modes of enquiry. However, the development of categorial orders and theoretical frameworks oriented toward normative objectives, grounded in terms of neo-functionalist properties demands reconsideration. The utilisation of such categorial orders as a means of ameliorating professional practice is distinct from the Parsonian concern with actually describing social practices. The manner through which Parsons' plenum re-emerges within the accounts of multidisciplinarity and team work illustrates the extent to which structural functionalist arguments remain intact and inform the formulation of models, through which professionals working within the field of activities described as social policy, have sought to implement.

In terms of situated studies and the operationalisation of empirical principles to applied problems, within the domain of social policy and administration, a situated approach could begin to examine the range of methods that members deploy in carrying out work activities. Furthermore, situated studies *could* provide an empirical *corpus* through which recommendations and procedures for carrying out specific tasks can be designed in a way that is sensitive to the features and characteristics of human interaction. As opposed to developing recommendations and procedures that are arrived at through the practice of theorising.

Respecifying the Concept of Institutions through a Situated Approach

The sociological investigation and analysis of institutions is one that has sought to trace the emergence of modern institutions and seek to explain both the causes and effects of institutional practices and organisation within modern societies. In many respects, the view of institutions as entities which were realised through complex, impersonal socio-historical forces was initially undermined by the interactionist approaches to the investigation of social institutions. Erving Goffman's studies of 'total institutions' were of particular significance in drawing attention to the way in which total institutions and the life world within them were the product of members interaction and presentation of 'self' within the context of institutional parameters. The significance of Goffman's work for the de-institutionalisation movement has been seen to be of extreme importance. Further analysis and observational work of members situated practices within institutional contexts may illuminate the almost infinite range of situated methods that members use in locally accomplishing a *sense* of institutional order. In this sense, an action model of organisations (Silverman,1970) is consistent with the concerns above, indeed it may be argued that a situated approach to institutions as an aspect of the action model of organisations represents a neglected, yet powerful, analytic approach to the understanding of institutional and organisational life. Clearly, some analysts may wish to explore multidisciplinarity in terms of its organisational contexts. However, an investigation into its situated dynamics and micro-sociological characteristics provides the means to respecify system based accounts and recommendations concerning multidisciplinary practice in teams.

Social Policy as an Interactive/Discursive Activity

The adoption of a situated approach within social policy studies would also provide an opportunity to investigate the activity of social policy as an interactive and discursive activity. As has been stated above, the notion that structures and institutions are the social dynamic through which the activities, associated with the field of social policy, are realised is to ignore the situated specifics of these activities. The emergence of Foucauldian theory within the human sciences has sensitised analysts to the linguistic credentials of power/knowledge and the discursive constitution of the subject within different regimes of truth. For Foucault, (1973) institutions such as the asylum was the product of particular practices constituted within the prevailing graph of power knowledge. The madmen, the vagrant and prisoner were particular discursive constructions which language, as discourse, impressed upon the body.

However, despite the adoption of the 'linguistic turn' within some approaches to the investigation of the field of social policy and administration, the examination of the conversational practices and interactional work in accomplishing social policy as both discourse and practice has been relatively unfocussed. The examination of policy and practice could take on board situated analyses as a means of investigating the ways through which *discourse is locally produced* within social policy settings. Furthermore, the vague notion of discourse could benefit from a consideration of ethnomethodological studies that, through thick description, provide an illustration of the methods and strategies that members deploy in carrying out activities associated with the field of study. The notion that the field of social policy should be examined solely in terms of historical accounts appears to be limiting. The investigation of the evolution of institutions and a consideration of the legislation and structural apparatus that deliver social policies is to ignore the wider developments within the human sciences and the benefits that the use of other approaches to the investigation of the field of social policy might provide. A focus on the situated contingencies of language and members activities within relevant contexts would, as this book has illustrated, draw attention to the way in which activities, taking place within the field of social policy settings, underpin generalised descriptions. Whilst normative concerns could be discussed on their own terms, the actual ways through which such concerns might be realised would benefit from the examination of the situated accomplishment of social order by members. The respecification of social policy in terms of locally achieved linguistic activities would draw attention to the way in which process (*i.e. members practical activities*), as opposed to structure, is the principle dynamic in delivering care, making decisions and organising work. Furthermore, as has been stated, the institutional 'thinking' of social policy discourse could be respecified in such a way that the accomplishment of such parameters would be available to normative consideration by those theorists wishing to tackle the totalising features of implicit functionalist thinking and practice.

In terms of the argument presented above, it must be noted that work on multidisciplinarity and teams has not stood still. An important development within studies of multidisciplinary teams in social and health care settings can be found in the work of Elwyn, Rapport and Kinnersley (1998:194). Drawing from the work of Hammer and Champey (1993) on team and role organisation in corporations, but working within a health context, they suggest that multidisciplinary Primary Health Care Teams should be re-engineered in order to provide a framework through which patients needs can be met more flexibly, accessibly and quickly in a climate where:

> ... the individual's role evolves from one that is narrow and task oriented to one that is multidimensional.

It is argued that this form of re-engineering within teams will help alleviate some of the problems outlined previously in this proposal including the areas specified by West and Slater (1996) and the general aims of multidisciplinarity. The notion of re-engineering is one that has a high degree of credence within private enterprise. The notion that models of team work require reconsideration is one that is both interesting and relevant. However, if re-engineering is taken to mean further structural functionalist theorising and modification I fear that some of the problems with team structures and practices (in terms of what they are being measured against) will remain. However, a broader and more radical reconceptualisation of team work that would consider analyses of the practical methods through which teamwork is accomplished and organised will provide further resources for pursuing the re-engineering of roles and other 'structures' within multidisciplinary contexts. To this extent the achievement of multidimensionality of roles (and the associated themes of knowledge and communicative structures and specific forms of interaction e.g. decision making) within teams would benefit form a consideration of the various methodical practices that members utilise in locally organising and achieving positions where interactional resources such as role are used. Thus, a consideration of research into actual team interaction and practices within such contexts should be viewed as an important appendage to the emerging agenda oriented to the re-engineering of roles and team structures within multidisciplinary and health care settings. Furthermore, this consideration is one that would benefit from standard and contemporary sociological reflections of structural functionalist theorising and model construction that still haunt policy formulation.

The Situated Approach and Resistance

A situated approach to examining social policy could provide a space through which normative concerns could be reconsidered. As I have stated, such concerns should not be confused with the process of describing the world although those wishing to tackle ethical, political and moral considerations will use such descriptions. The adoption of a situated approach for the examination of social policy has resonance with the Foucauldian concern with 'micro-politics'. For Foucault, the unity of purpose espoused by the universal categories of 'truth', 'justice', 'principles' and 'emancipatory interests' had little relevance to the experiences of tactical alliances and the emergence of competing groups and positions within the leftist movement during 1968. This observation was coupled with Foucault's critiques of the universal claims of the Enlightenment project and the emergence of disciplinary forms of power knowledge. For Foucault (1977: 211,116), the disciplinary knowledge of the institution is one of the features of the totalising tendencies of the modern. Furthermore:

> ... the mechanisms (of the disciplinary establishments) have a certain tendency to become 'de-institutionalised,' to emerge from the closed fortresses in which they once functioned and to circulate in a 'free' state; the massive, compact disciplines are broken down into flexible methods of control, which may be transferred and adapted ... One can (therefore) speak of the formation of a disciplinary society in this movement that stretches from the enclosed disciplines, a sort of 'quarantine,' to an indefinitely generalisable mechanism of "panapoticism".

The notion that disciplinary power, developed and organised within institutions, is beginning to circulate within the social body is one which has resonance within the human sciences (Donzelot 1973). However, from a situated perspective (one which is primarily ethical rather than sociological in character) Foucault urges the practice of local resistance to the imposition of disciplinary practice and the spectre of totalising discourse. For Foucault, the practice of constant critique is one way to combat disciplinary knowledge, as is the development of situated practices that resist the process of categorisation, labelling and interpolation into specific ways of speaking dictated by the internal logicity of totalising discourse. Foucault's conceptualisation of the social is very much expressed in terms of structural metaphors. However, Foucault observed that the social body was characterised by 'micro-capillaries' through which power/knowledge was realised. Foucault's concern with micro-politics rested on a description of the way in which ethics could be approached in a situated manner, as opposed to an appeal to the discredited notion of universal truth which would be substituted by a highly situated locally-specific resistance to the totalising tendencies of the disciplining effects of modernist discourse. As Christopher Norris states (1994:187), with respect to the Foucauldian recommendation of adopting a situated position:

> What the times thus required was a flexible attitude, a readiness to abandon high-sounding talk of "truth", "principles", "justice", "emancipatory interests", or whatever, and a corresponding will to bend all one's energies to various short-term "specific" projects of localised resistance and critique. Insofar as such projects stood in need of justification, it could be only be a matter of pointing out their strategic usefulness in pursuit of some goal whose desirability was simply self - evident to those pursuing it, but whose ultimate good could never be determined with reference to higher ("universal" or "transcendent") grounds of ethical judgement.

The notion of situated ethics and resistance may be viewed as notions that are theoretical recommendations for meeting normative concerns. However, whether or not such recommendations are theoretical (in the sense of traditional modes of sociological theorising) they are of importance to a situated approach in that they can be read in such a way as to reflect the observational findings of ethnomethodological enquiry. This is not to say that Foucauldian ethical concerns are commensurable with the concerns of thick description, however the examination of talk within this study has illustrated the way in which a sense of social order or discourse are the product of members situated work. It *might* be argued that Foucauldian ideas and ethnomethodology should be married in order to develop an apparatus through which the situated character of social life can be more fully accounted for and ethically challenged by those wishing to cope with the post modern condition. This combination of approaches may be viewed and promoted as a way that does not fully reject certain enlightenment notions and resists the increasing surveillance, control and bio-power of disciplinary power/knowledge and techno-social practices. *I disagree*, a concern with situated practices should present itself not as a coherent position but as a collection of concerns, within which observation and thick description are presented as different forms of life and activities from the consideration of situated ethics or micro-political resistance to local forms of discipline and control. However, whilst the normative remains within this position theorising becomes a redundant practice in that situated analyses rely on observing particular instances of action. The co-flation of situated analyses with the post-structuralist call for a situated ethic and resistance to the totalising and disciplinary features of the modern may appear to be strange. However, the call for situated resistance to totalising discourse and the ethnomethodological stem from a rejection of the notion of totality. The situated ethic is a rejection of the validity of totalising narratives (the grand narratives of the modernist epoch). This rejection is the result of a range of critiques and historical accounts, these accounts have identified the totalising features of discourse as the means through which the new barbarism of the twentieth century emerged. The notions of universal truth and common humanity were undermined as the bomb, the gulag and the holocaust compromised the faith in rational progress.

The rejection of totalisation within *situated analysis* stems from an *empirical* consideration rather than the *ethical* questions raised through the accounts of people recalling recent events in history (*important as they are*). For ethnomethodologists, traditional sociological enquiry treats members as 'judgmental dopes'. For Garfinkel, professional sociologists and members of society construct a sense of the world in much the same way. As Garfinkel (1967:75) states:

> (Analysis) is not the monopoly of philosophers and professional sociologists. Members of the society are concerned as a matter of course and necessarily with these matters both as features and for the socially managed production of their everyday affairs. The study of common sense knowledge and common sense activities consists of treating as problematic phenomena the actual methods whereby members of a society, doing sociology, lay or professional, make the social structures of everyday activities observable.

This observation by Garfinkel represents an empirical stance against the facticity of the totalising accounts of the social. For Garfinkel, the notion that the social was accomplished through a variety of systemic processes and institutional functions was to ignore the empirical and observable manner through which members accomplished the social. From this position, the totalising narratives produced through the practices of theorising about the world were merely, in terms of the documentary method of interpretation, further members versions of accounting for the social by pointing to and invoking underlying patterns. The notion that the social could be explained in terms of an all embracing grand unified theory was to completely miss the haecceity and locally produced and situated character of social life.

Thus, whilst the concerns of a situated ethics and situated analyses directed towards the investigation and consideration of activities conventionally located within the field of social policy are distinct. They may be understood to have co-relevance through the rejection of totalising approaches, accounts and versions of the social but they remain incommensurable in the sense that situated *analysis* (as exemplified through ethnomethodological work) has no interest in promoting a normative conceptualisation of the world situated or otherwise. Having established this point, even if the ethnomethodological programme embarked on such an enterprise how could an 'ethic' be both situated as an embedded feature of members' practical activities and universal at one and the same time? Is it not the case that the very process of using situated ethics as a means of resisting totalising discourse is inexorably and inevitably reflexively constituted by the parameters, conditions and characteristics that it seeks to overcome? However, if all resistance to totalising discourse must be situated (so as to avoid the totalitarian effects of such discourse) then the thick description of members *situated* activities seems a good way of carrying out such concerns. To describe and *account* for members' practical activities (including professional sociological theorising) is to engage in a reflexive practice. The activity of reflecting and reflexively describing the world and the methods for accomplishing a sense of the world resists the totalising features of members accounts by explicating and illustrating the very practices that produced such orderly phenomenon in the first place. Through the consideration of members activities (including professional social scientists) the process of turning resources into topics of enquiry in their own right *could* be construed as resistance to any *narrative, theory* or *discourse* from policing a full stop.

Multidisciplinarity and Real Lives

Within the course of this book the mundane work of doing 'the team' has been explored within the context of multidisciplinarity. The book has related such issues to questions of role, knowledge, narrative and discourse, epistemology, rationality and communication. However, at the heart of this concern with documenting the detailed practices of multidisciplinary team work is a concern that such sites and settings process the lives of others and organise and produce social effects in localised sites, settings, communities and environments. An understanding of the character of such settings and social technology is crucial in beginning to chart the various forms of people processing apparatus that is increasingly to be found inhabiting and colonising the life world. Ethnomethodology, whilst indifferent to these normative principles, provides a clear analytical means through which to document such processes and effects. Furthermore, with other work that is being carried out in similar settings the suspicion that the rational properties of social amelioration are riddled with interstitial spaces of lay reasoning, commonsense accounts, hunches, mundane heirarchies and other activities renders visible the contestable character of the work of micro-organisations in the processing of vulnerable groups. Indeed, whilst an appreciation of the social organisation of such settings may aid professional development via reflexive practice, or provide material through which team organisation can be 're-engineered' it also provides the means and the opportunity to question the taken for granted rationality of people processing. Indeed, it may provide grounds for resistance and critical scrutiny of such forms of organisation that routinely constitute and process real lives utilising mundane resources and practical reasoning that is consistent with and no more superior to any other order of ordinary action. Indeed, the claim that such activities are of a higher order than other forms of practical reasoning, is not, in this case, borne out through observation nor analytical investigation. To this extent whilst this book does provide a resource for professionals and does provide some grounds for developing the action model of organisations, with a view to re-engineering micro-institutions and larger organisations, it can also be understood to provide an alternate lense through which people processing can be viewed as a mundane array of practical methods of reasoning, organising and doing the days work that have real and lasting effects upon peoples lives. To this extent this book is not an exercise in social philosophy but an ethnomethodological ethnography of hidden practices.

Bibliography

Atkinson, M.A., Cuff, E.C. and Lee, J.R.E. (1978), 'The Recommencement of a Meeting as Member's Accomplishment', in J. Schenkein (ed.) *Language, Thought and Culture: Advances in the Study of Cognition*, Academic Press, London, pp.133-54.

Baker, C.D. (1984), The search for adultness: membership work in adolescent-adult talk, *Human Studies*, 7, pp.301-23.

Bauman, R. (1986), *Story, performance and event: Contextual studies of oral narrative*, Cambridge University Press, Cambridge.

Belbin, R.M. (1981), *Management teams*, Butterworth Heinemann, Oxford.

Boden, D. and Zimmerman, D.H. (eds) (1992) *Talk and Social Structure*, Polity Press, Oxford.

Bourdieu, P. (1990), *Reproduction in education, society and culture*, Sage Publications, London.

Brill, N.I. (1976), *Teamwork: Working Together in the Helping Services*, J.B. Lippincott co., Philadelphia.

Butrym Z. and Horder, J. (1983), *Health Doctors and Social Work*, Macmillan Education, Basingstoke.

Button, G. (ed.) (1991), *Ethnomethodology and the Human Sciences*, Cambridge University Press, Cambridge.

Clarke, J. and Sapsford, R. (1994), *A Crisis in Care,* Sage Publications, London.

Coffey, A. and Atkinson, P. (1996), *Making Sense of Qualitative Data*, Sage Publications, London.

Cortazzi, M. (1993), *Narrative Analysis*, Falmer, London.

Coulon, A. (1995), *Ethnomethodology*, Sage Publications, London.

Coulshead, V. (1991), *Management in Social Work*, Macmillan Education, Basingstoke.

Coulter, J. (1979), 'Beliefs and Practical Understanding', in G. Psathas (ed.), *Everyday Language*, Irvington Press, New York.

Coulter, J. (1983), 'Contingent and *A Priori* Structures in Sequential Analysis', *Human Studies*, 6, p.4.

Coulthard, M. (1977), *An Introduction to Discourse Analysis*, Longman, London.

Donnison, J. (1977), *Midwives and medical men a history of inter-professional rivalries and womens rights,* Heinemann Educational, London.

Donzelot, J. (1973), *The Policing of Families,* Macmillan, London.

Drew, P. (1978), 'Accusations: the occasioned use of members' knowledge of "religous geography" in describing events', *Sociology*, 12.

Drew, P. and Heritage, J. (1992), *Talk at Work: interaction in institutional settings,* Cambridge University Press, Cambridge.

Eglin, P. and Hester, S. (1992), Category, predicate and task: the pragmatics of practical action, Semiotica 8-3/4, pp.243-68.

Elwyn, J.E., Rapport, F. and Kinnersley, P. (1998), 'Primary health care teams re-engineered', *Journal of Interprofessional Care*, 12, 2, pp.189-97.

Everitt, A. (1992), *Applied Research for Better Practice*, Macmillan, Basingstoke.

Evers H. (1981), 'Multidisciplinary Teams in Geriatric Wards: Myth or Reality', *Journal of Advanced Nursing* 1981, 6, pp.205-14.

Fevre, R. and Thompson, A. (eds) (1999), *Nation, Identity and Social Theory: Perspectives from Wales*, University of Wales Press, Cardiff.

Field, R. and West, M. (1995), 'Teamwork in primary health care: perspectives from practices', *Journal of Interprofessional Care*, 9, 2, pp.30-123.

Foucault, M. (1973), *Birth of the Clinic*, Tavistock, London.

Foucault, M. (1976, 1977), *Discipline and Punishment: The Birth of the Prison*, Trans. A.M. Sheridean – Smith, Vintage/Random House.

Fuller, R. and Petch, A. (1995), *Practitioner Research: The Reflexive Social Worker*, Open University Press, Buckingham.

Garfinkel, H. (1967), *Studies in Ethnomethodology*, Polity Press, Cambridge.

Gibbons, M. et al (1994), The New Production of Knowledge, *The Dynamics of Science and Research in Contemporary Societies*, Sage Publications, London.

Glastonbury, B., Bradley, R. and Orme, J. (1987), *Managing People in the Personal Social Services*, Wiley series, New York.

Goffman, E. (1967), *Asylums, Essays on the Social situation of Mental Patients and Other Inmates*, Penguin.

Goodwin, C. (1981), *Conversational Organisation: Interaction Between Speakers*, Academic Press, New York.

Guzzo, R.A. and Shea, G.P. (1992), 'Group Performance and inter-relations in organisations', in M.D. Dunnete and L.M. Hough (eds), *Handbook of industrial and organisational psychology*, Consulting Psychologists Press, 3, pp.269-313.

Habermas, J. (1990), *The Theory of Communicative Action*, 2: System and Lifeworld: A Critique of Functionalist reason, Polity Press, Cambridge.

Halkowski, T. (1990), 'Role' as an interactional device, *Social Problems*, 37 pp.564–77.

Hammer, M. and Champey, J. (1993), *Re-engineering the corporation: a manifesto for business revolution*, Business Books, London.

Hammersley, M. and Atkinson, P. (1995), *Ethnography: Principles and Practice*, Routledge, London.

Hester, S. (1992), 'Recognising References to Deviance in Referral Talk', in Watson and Smieler (eds), *Text in Context*, Sage Publications, London, pp.156-74.

Hester, S. (1994), Les categories en contexte. *Raisons Pratiques* (5) pp.219-42, Special Issues title 'L'Entquite sur les Categories: de Durkheim et Sacks', (eds.), B.Fradin, L.Quèrè and J.Widmer. Editions de l'Ecole des Hautes Etudes en Sciences Sociales, Paris.

Hester, S. and Eglin, P. (1997), *Culture in Action: Studies in Membership Categorization Analysis*, International Institute for Ethnomethodology and Conversation Analysis and University Press of America, Washington, D.C.

Hester, S. and Francis, D. (1994), 'Doing data: the local organization of a sociological interview', *British Journal of Sociology*, 45, 4, pp.675-95.

Hester, S. and Francis, D. (2000), Institutional Talk Institutionalised?, *TEXT*, 20, 1.

Hester, S. and Francis, D. (forthcoming). *The Institutional Talk Programme: Ethnomethodology Institutionalised?*

Hester, S. and Housley, W. (2002), *Language, Interaction and National Identity*, Ashgate, Aldershot.

Hey, (1979), in Marshall et al (1979), *Teamwork: For and Against*, BASW Publications, Birmingham, p.25.

Hilbert (1981), in T. Halkowski (1990), 'Role as an interactional device', *Social Problems*, 37, pp.564-77.

HMSO (1959), *Report of the Working Party on Social Workers in Local Authority Health and Welfare Services*, HMSO.

Housley, W. (1999), 'Role as an Interactional Resource and Device within Multidisciplinary Team Meetings', *Sociological Research Online*, 4, 3.

Housley, W. (2000a), 'Category Work and Knowlegeability within Multi-disciplinary Team Meetings', *TEXT*, 20, 1.

Housley, W. (2000b), 'Story, Narrative and Teamwork', *The Sociological Review*, 48, 3.

Housley, W. and Fitzgerald, R. (2000), 'Conversation Analysis, Practitioner Based Research, Reflexivity and Reflective Practice: Some Exploratory Remarks', *Ethnographic Studies*, Autumn, 5.

Housley, W. and Fitzgerald, R. (2002), The Reconsidered Model of Membership Categorisation Analysis. Qualitative Research (awaiting issue).

Hunt. E. and Marshall, T. (1977), in Marshall et al (1979), *Teamwork: For and Against*, BASW Publications, Birmingham, p.15.

Jacques, P. (1978) in Glastonbury, Bradley and Orme (1987), *Managing People in the Personal Social Services*, Wiley series, New York, p.47.

Jayussi, L. (1991), 'Values and Moral Judgement', in *Ethnomethodology and the Human Sciences,* G. Button (ed.), Cambridge University Press, Cambridge, pp.227-51.

Jefferson, G. (1978), 'Sequential aspects of storytelling in conversation', in J. Schenkein (ed.), *Studies in the organisation of conversational interaction*, Academic Press, New York, pp.219-48.

Kline, S.J. (1995), *Conceptual foundations for multidisciplinary thinking*, Stanford University Press, Stanford.

Levinson, S.C. (1994), *Pragmatics*, Cambridge University Press, Cambridge.

Lynch, M. and Bogen, D. (1996), *The Spectacle of History, Speech, Text and Memory at the Iran-Contra Hearings*, Duke University Press, Durham and London.

McGrath, P. (1991), *Multidisciplinary Teamwork. Community Mental Handicap Teams in Wales,* Centre for Social Policy Research and Development, University College of North Wales, Bangor.

McHoul, A. and Watson, D.R. (1984), 'Two axes for the analysis of "commonsense" and "formal" geographical knowledge in classroon talk', *British Journal of the Sociology of Education*, 5, 3.

Norris, C. (1993). "What is enlightenment?"; Kant according to Foucault in *The Cambridge Companion to Foucault* (ed. Gary Gutting), Cambridge University Press, Cambridge.

NHSME (1993), *Nursing in Primary Care – New World, New Opportunities,* NHSME, Leeds.

Øvretveit J. (1994), *Coordinating community care: Multidisciplinary teams and care management*, Open University Press, Buckingham.

Parsons, T (1956), *The Social System*, Tavistock, London.

Pearson, P. and Spencer, J. (1995), 'Pointers to effective teamwork: Exploring primary care', *Journal of Interprofessional Care*, 9, 2, pp.131-38.

Pearson, P. and Van Zwanberg, T. (1991), *Who is the primary health care team? What should they be doing?*, University of Newcastle, Department of Primary Care, Newcastle upon Tyne.

Pomerantz A. (1978), 'Compliment Responses: Notes on the Co-operation of Multiple Constraints', in J. Schenkein (ed.) *Language, Thought and Culture: Advances in the Study of Cognition*, Academic Press, London.

Pomerantz, A.M. (1978), 'Attributions of Responsibility: Blamings', *Sociology*, 12.

Preston, R.J. (1978), *Cree narrative: Expressing the personal meanings of events*, Canadian Ethnology Service, Ottawa.

Psathas, G. (1995), *Conversation Analysis: The Study of Talk-in – Interaction,* Sage Publications, London.

Ramcharan, P. (1993), *An Evaluation of aspects of the social organization of Case Selection in a Community Mental Health Centre,* (unpublished Ph.D thesis).

Sacks, H., Schegloff, E.A. and Jefferson, G. (1974), *A simplest systematics for the organization of turn taking for conversation*, Language, 50, pp.697-735.

Salvage, A.V. (1985), *Future for the Elderly: a response to the Welsh Office initiative*, St David's Hospital, Cardiff.

Sapsford, R in J. Clarke and R. Sapsford (1995), *A Crisis in Care*, Sage Publications, London.

Schegloff, E.A. (1992), Introduction, in H. Sacks, *Lectures in Conversation Vol.1* (1992), ix-lxii.

Schenkein, J. (ed.) (1978), *Studies in the organisation of conversational interaction*, Academic Press, New York.

Schön, D. (1991), *The reflective Practitioner: How Professionals Think in Action*, Arena, Ashgate Publishing, Aldershot.

Sharrock, W.W. (1974), 'On Owning Knowledge' in R. Turner (ed.), *Ethnomethodology*, Penguin Education, Penguin Books, Middlesex, 9, pp. 45-53.

Silverman, D. (1970), *Theory of Organisations: A Sociological Framework*, Heinemann, London.

Silverman, D. (1998), *Harvey Sacks: Social Science and Conversation Analysis*, Polity Press, Oxford.

Stoddart, K. (1974), 'Pinched: Notes on the Ethnographer's Location of Argot' in R. Turner (ed.) *Ethnomethodology*, Penguin Education, Middlesex, 9, pp.173-77.

Tolkeon, J.B. (1975), 'Folklore, world view and communication' in D. Ben-Amos and K.S. Goldstein (eds.), *Folklore, performance and communication*, Mouton, The Hague, pp.265-86.

Tucker, K.H. (1998), *Anthony Giddens and Modern Social Theory*, Polity Press, Oxford.

Van Dijk, TA. (1997), *Discourse as Social Interaction*, Sage Publications, London.

Watson, D.R. (1978), 'Categorisation, Authorisation and Blame Negotiation in Conversation', *Sociology*, 12, 1, pp.105-13.

Watson, D.R. (1983), The Presentation of Victim and Offender in Discourse: The Case of Police Interrogations and Interviews, *Victimology*, 8, 1/2.

Watson, D.R. (1997), 'Some general reflections of category and sequence', in Hester and Eglin (eds.) *Culture in Action: Studies in Membership Categorization Analysis*, International Institute for Ethnomethodology and Conversation Analysis and University Press of America, Washington D.C., pp.49-75.

West, M. (1994), *Effective teamwork*, The British Psychological Society, Leceister.

West, M.A. and Slater, J. (1996), *Teamworking in Primary Care: A Review of its Effectiveness*, HEA, London.

Wittgenstein, L. (1968 [1958]), *Philosophical Investigations*, Blackwell, Oxford.

Wood, N., Farrow, S. and Eliot, B. (1994), 'A review of primary health care organisation', *Journal of Clinical Nursing*, 3, 4, 243-50.

Index